ECCENTRICS

for Andy,
our Greatest Friend
with love from

ECCENTRICS

John and
Victoria

John Jolliffe

Duckworth

First published in 2001 by
Gerald Duckworth & Co. Ltd.
61 Frith Street, London W1D 3JL
Tel: 020 7434 4242
Fax: 020 7434 4420
Email: inquiries@duckworth-publishers.co.uk
www.ducknet.co.uk

Extract from *A Spaniard in the Works* by John Lennon published by
Jonathan Cape. Used by permission of The Random House Group Limited.

Extract from *The Pendulum Years* by Bernard Levin (Jonathan Cape, 1970)
reproduced by kind permission of Curtis Brown on behalf of Bernard Levin.
© Bernard Levin 1970.

Every effort has been made to contact copyright holders; in the event of
any omission or error, the editorial department should be notified at
61 Frith Street, London W1D 3JL.

A catalogue record for this book is available
from the British Library

ISBN 0 7156 3050 4

Illustration credits in order of appearance: Colonel Charles de Waldo
Sibthorpe reproduced by kind permission of Mary Evans Picture Library;
Charles Waterton from a painting by Charles Wilson Peale, reproduced
by kind permission of Mary Evans Picture Library; John Christie by Guy
Gravett, reproduced by kind permission of the Glyndebourne Archive;
William Beckford by Sir Joshua Reynolds, reproduced by kind
permission of Mary Evans Picture Library; William Blake by W.C.
Edwards, reproduced by kind permission of Mary Evans Picture Library;
Sir George Reresby Sitwell reproduced by kind permission of Hulton
Archive; Edward Lear by Edward Lear, reproduced by kind permission
of Mary Evans Picture Library; Lewis Carroll reproduced by kind
permission of Mary Evans Picture Library; Lady Hester Lucy Stanhope
reproduced by kind permission of Hulton Archive; Victoria Woodhull
reproduced by kind permission of Hulton Archive; Sir Iain Moncreiffe
reproduced by kind permission of *The Field*

Typeset by Derek Doyle & Associates, Liverpool
Printed and bound in Great Britain by
Bookcraft (Bath) Ltd, Midsomer Norton, Avon

For Hugh Montgomery-Massingberd

Contents

Introduction

Eccentricity is the condition of being regulated by no central control, of being 'irregular, odd, capricious, whimsical'. In the eyes of most of us, a little eccentricity goes a long way, and too much of it soon becomes tedious. So if an eccentric is to be a rewarding and attractive character, as opposed to a bore, he or she must exert some degree of self-discipline, or at least have some non-eccentric qualities. Moreover, if it is self-conscious, or studied, eccentricity soon becomes off-putting. The characters described in the book, as opposed to those briefly mentioned, on the whole pass this test. Coleridge or Beau Brummell would fail.

I have excluded men and women who were completely mad, or incapable of directing their words and actions rationally; though this state may often be interspersed with lucid intervals, which may include flashes of great inspiration. Addicts to drink, drugs and gambling are to be pitied, not mocked or laughed at, but they are often of interest. When all else failed, the Victorian gambler Benzon, known as the Jubilee Juggins after a disastrous day at Kempton Park, wrote a book called *How I Lost a Million and a Quarter in Two Years*. It would be a dull story, were it not that he fairly frequently made extremely profitable bets, so that hope unfortunately sprang eternal, to the end of his brief career.

Then there are those whose eccentricities are contrived, often resulting from a desire to give an impression that they are more interesting than they really are; from a craving for sympathy, affection and even admiration, often to compensate for disadvantages, real or imagined, suffered in early life, or wrongs inflicted on them later: lack of appreciation or love, uncomplimentary comparisons with siblings, downright bullying, or the loss of a much-loved home. Their behaviour, like that of the addicts, is also more to be pitied, however tiresome it may be. Compulsive misers are in another category which soon palls. The American banker George Peabody, who generously spent half a million pounds on providing tolerable housing conditions for the poor in London in the 1870s, would stand waiting in the rain outside his bank, waiting for a penny bus to come along, rather than one which would cost him twopence. More fool him, one is tempted to say.

There is a large category of people about whom one or two delightful anecdotes have survived, but do not bear examining at any length. Lady Cumming-Bruce, wife of a High Commissioner in New Zealand, whose interest in landscape painting greatly exceeded her punctiliousness as a hostess, is one example. She was regularly to be seen arriving late for her own garden parties, emerging on all fours from the bushes at the edge of the large lawn on which her guests were awaiting her, rather than the other way round. There was Colonel Maurice Willoughby, whose eventful career was going to be the subject of a television series. When his producer rang to check the time of the next day's filming, he explained that he had had 'a spot of bad luck'. Expecting an accident or a broken limb, the producer inquired sympathetically what it had been. 'The wife died yesterday, I'm afraid,' was the answer. 'But don't worry, I'll be there.'

Eccentrics also tend to attract coincidences. Colonel Sir George ('Loopy') Kennard found himself, with a small part of his regiment, with their backs to the sea at Salonika in 1941, in the face of the advancing Germans. Pausing to look after a wounded brother officer, he was surprised to hear himself addressed by someone speaking English in a German accent which he recognised. It was a member of a German family that he had known well before the war. Each fluent in the other's language, they acted as go-betweens and organised the surrender of some 10,000 Allied troops who would otherwise have been pointlessly shelled to pieces on the beaches.

Eccentricity often becomes more marked in old age, as people become less affected by what others may think of them. The irrepressible Lady Oxford, better known as Margot Asquith, once caused surprise by announcing that 'King George V told me himself that he would never have died if Sir Thomas Barlow had treated him properly'. But it is often exceptional quick-wittedness that makes people speak before thinking. Many years earlier, when her husband had been infatuated with his daughter's friend and contemporary, Venetia Stanley, the latter had apologised politely for having been such a frequent visitor at the Asquiths' house. Margot replied, 'Well, it has been rather a bore having you here all the time, but don't tell anyone I said so, darling.' And when someone praised F.E. Smith's wit, she commented, rather aptly, that 'Lord Birkenhead is very clever, but his brains have gone to his head'.

A great eccentric who I have left out with extreme reluctance is Frederick Hervey, the eighteenth-century Earl of Bristol and Bishop of Derry; had there not been an excellent recent biography of him by Brian Fothergill I would have described him at length. His good and bad points were equally remarkable.

As a young man at Cambridge, he was praised by a famous antiquary for his application to study which was 'as remarkable as it was unusual in persons of his rank'. As a young clergyman he was praised, by Wesley of all people, for a useful and judicious sermon on 'Blasphemy of the Holy Spirit', and by the Archbishop of Armagh for his theological erudition. In the diocese of Derry, he showed far more tolerance and friendliness to the Roman Catholic majority than any of his predecessors, or for that matter, than most of those who followed him. There was a time when he had to make an appointment to a particularly rich and desirable living and his method of selection was to invite all those who had applied to a sumptuous and prolonged dinner, at the end of which he led them out into a field, and told them to hold a race across it, with the winner to be awarded the living. He did not, however, mention that it contained, in the middle, a wide and deep bog. The hares set off at full tilt, while the tortoises were able to observe what was happening, and pursue a longer and more prudent course round the edge of the swamp.

When he came into the family estates the Bishop's public generosity in Derry was on a magnificent scale. He headed the list of subscribers to a new and splendid bridge over the Foyle with a personal contribution of £1000. He employed armies of workmen in the construction of roads in remote districts, he originated a pension scheme for the widows of rectors, and contributed to the building of chapels for both Roman Catholics and Dissenters almost as freely as to the churches of his own flock. He worked with Shelburne to promote the cause of parliamentary reform, declaring in 1788 his unshakeable purpose 'to liberate this high-mettled nation from the petulant and rapacious oligarchy which plunders and insults it'.

So far, so good, even though his language had become as violent as that of any Jacobin. But in 1792 he went into reverse, abandoning his liberal sentiments and indeed most of his episcopal duties. Who knows if he was sickened by the Terror in France, or disgusted by British policy in Ireland, or both? For whatever reason, he suddenly retired to Rome and gave full rein to his idiosyncracies. Miss Catherine Wilmot, in her account of 'An Irish Peer on the Continent' (published in 1920) described him as follows:

At the Bishop of Derry's house is an exhibition of the fine arts, we went to see it and were amused as well with the contents as the singularity of the arrangements. He is the patron of all modern artists, whose wives he not only associates with as his only female company but has their pictures drawn as Venuses all over the house. His three favourite mistresses are beautifully represented as Juno, Minerva and Venus in the Judgment of Paris. Tho' he is one of the greatest curiosities alive, yet such is his notorious character for profane conversation and so great a reprobate is he in the most unlicensed sense of the word that the English do not consider it a very creditable thing to be much in his society, excepting only when curiosity particularly prompts.

I have oft seen him riding and driving past our windows and his appearance is so very singular that I must describe him. His figure is tall and his face very sharp and wicked; on his head he wore a purple velvet nightcap with a tassel of god dangling over his shoulder and a sort of mitre to the front; silk stockings and slippers of the same colour, and a short round petticoat such as Bishops wear, fringed with gold about his knees. A loose dressing-gown of silk was then thrown about his shoulders. In this Merry Andrew trim he rode on horseback to the never ending amazement of all Beholders! The last time I saw him he was sitting in his carriage between two Italian women dressed in a white bed gown and a nightcap like a witch, and giving himself the airs of an Adonis.

The stories one hears of him are endless both in the line of immorality and irreligion and in general he manages to affront everyone he invites to his table. To counterbalance all this he admires the Arts, supports the Artists and spends such a quantity of money in Italy that amongst other rarities he has also purchased friends. However his residence at Rome has thoroughly confirmed the idea which most foreigners have of the English character being the most bizarre in the world – bizarre but generous.

Any selection of eccentrics is bound to be a personal one, and many books could be written on the subject without repeating one another.

I have disregarded, on the whole, tedious cranks and freaks, and have concentrated on men and women whose originality and energy were based on interesting ideas, or led to notable achievements – like those of John Christie – or simply led to and arresting way of life, as in the case of Lady Hester Stanhope or Squire Waterton. There may be complaints that those I have chosen were mostly more or less prosperous. The reason for this is that it is on the whole more entertaining to read about those who were in a position to indulge their fancies, anyway for a time, rather than about lesser and more brutal oddities.

This book is about English eccentrics (with one Scot thrown in). Otherwise it would be interminable. I have omitted Ireland, where it is eccentric *not* to be eccentric.

1

Charles and Richard Sibthorpe

(1783–1855 & 1792–1879)

Eccentrics being what they are, any attempt to classify them at all rigidly would be a waste of time. Nevertheless they seem to fall into a number of loose categories, which may be a help in explaining their actions to some extent.

My first group of eccentrics are the visionaries; men and women who dream impossible dreams, and follow unattainable will-o'-the-wisps. In doing so they lose sight of the criteria and priorities which guide more conventional people. One interesting case that occurred in the nineteenth century was that of two brothers, from a conventional land-owning background, who flew off, for no known reason, at two completely different tangents. One of the Sibthorpe brothers may already be known to students of the unusual, the other probably not.

Colonel Charles de Laet Waldo Sibthorpe – the name itself arouses high expectations – became in 1822 the head of a prosperous Lincolnshire family. He had served in the Peninsular Wars and become Colonel of the local militia. From 1827 to 1855 he sat in the House of Commons. His principles, and loyalties, were unshakeable by any change in circumstances, let alone by any new scientific discoveries. Above all, he believed in the sacred nature of the British Constitution, so far as anyone knew what it was. The passing of the Reform Act in 1832 deprived him of his seat in Parliament, though only very briefly: and such was his popularity that his female supporters presented him with an expensive diamond ring, as a mark of their personal esteem. In 1834 he was re-elected on a popular vote. But after this experience he was more on his guard than ever against the dreadful dangers of innovation. His first obsession was with the vital need to protect the throne from interference by foreign princes, in a sacredly English England. His basic ideas survive today, in however diluted a form, in the highly rational fears of the Eurosceptics about the creeping control of their country by unelected officials in Brussels, answerable only to one another. But so far from being, like them, concerned with wider issues such as levels of unemployment and social benefits, or taxation, or the survival of farmers and fishermen, or the danger of homosexual proselytising in schools, the Colonel had narrower targets in his sights. His appearance was described in Fraser's Magazine in 1847 as 'the debris of what must once have been a magnifico. A majestic air of tawdry grandeur', and in the House of Commons he appeared in a bottle-green frock coat and a tall white hat. He was also described as looking 'rather as Murat might have looked when he found the game was up in Naples', or Goering on his arrest in 1945. But for the Colonel the game was never up. However absurd his frequent interjections in the House of Commons, however wild the personal abuse which he showered on his enemies, he was never called to order, never asked to withdraw his enormities, but was regularly greeted with roars of delighted laughter. In some odd way, he never became a bore. He was an outrageous breath of fresh air, an echo of which can perhaps be traced to the late Alan Clark, though the latter's verbal excesses were sometimes specifically designed to annoy, whereas the Colonel's were entirely natural and spontaneous. He instinctively opposed every clause in the Catholic Emancipation Bill, but when his brother joined the Catholic Church, it did nothing to damage the excellent terms which they were on. He 'had a clear vision of his own duty, but performed it without rancour towards others'.

Nor did he always intervene in vain. His greatest positive achievement, however unintentional, arose in 1845. Horrified by the size of the annuity that had been voted to the Prince Consort, he moved that it should be reduced from £50,000 to £30,000 a year. To everyone's amazement, including that of the Colonel, Peel, who as leader of the Opposition had not been consulted about the amount, seconded the motion, defeated the Government, and set in motion the political decline of its Leader, Lord Melbourne. Queen Victoria, outraged, refused to set foot in Lincoln while Sibthorpe continued to represent it.

Catholic Emancipation was chronologically the first of his bugbears, followed closely by the Reform Bill and the person of Lord John Russell. Worse still was the coming of the railways. He looked to the day when 'the steam engine would vanish as an evil dream'. Dostoevsky is known to have studied British parliamentary reports, and it is not unlikely that he had the Colonel in mind when he created the character of Lebedev in *The Idiot*, with his own crazy moral obsessions. Sibthorpe also accused the railway companies of suppressing details of accidents, understating the number of casualties, and even denying that accidents had occurred. One of his few other successes was in preventing the Great Northern Railway from coming to Lincoln, to the displeasure of some of his more adventurous constituents. And he predicted that 'soon all the railway companies would be bankrupt and that the old and happy mode of travelling the turnpike roads, in chaises, carriages and stages, would be restored'. The first half of his prediction has come to pass in a sense, and motor coaches are increasingly preferred to trains. So perhaps the Colonel was not so far off the mark after all.

The score at this stage was Sibthorpe 1, Prince Consort nil. But the Prince was to have his revenge over the Great Exhibition of 1851, which Sibthorpe denounced as 'one of the greatest humbugs, [a favourite term of abuse] one of the greatest frauds, one of the greatest absurdities ever known'. He was horrified to see trees being cut down in Hyde Park, good English trees, to make way for 'this palace of tomfoolery ... this unwholesome castle of glass'. He prayed God to strike it down with hailstones or lightning. Above all, the Colonel gave the following warning, well expressed by Christopher Sykes in *Two Studies in Virtue* (1953):

> He warned the House that the Exhibition would tempt foreigners to visit these shores. He described their object in so doing as four-fold: to undersell, to burgle, to rape and chiefly to spy. He had always mistrusted Prince Albert on account of his foreign birth (conveniently passing over the rest of the royal family since 1714) and he saw now the climax of a treacherous career: the entice-ment of other foreigners to London in order to disturb our English peace. He always spoke as if the hatefulness of foreigners (hypocritical foreigners as he always called them) was an agreed fact, not worth argument or illustration, because self-evident.

The bankruptcy of the nation was another disaster confidently predicted by Sibthorpe, even though expanding trade and Empire were in the process of making Britain the most prosperous of coun-tries. But he believed that the country could certainly not afford the Royal Commissions set up to investigate possible reforms, nor could it afford to pay British diplomats abroad, who he felt should give their services for nothing. And in spite of being a connoisseur, with a fine collection of paintings and classical antiquities at home, he opposed the building of the National Gallery, and even suggested, when it was nearly completed, that it should be pulled down to avoid further expense.

However wild Sibthorpe's xenophobia, what makes it interesting today is that it can be traced back at least as far as the days of the Spanish Armada, and perhaps to the Danes. What he would have thought of the Channel Tunnel does not bear considering. But it seems likely that until the North Sea and the English Channel dry up, his fears will never quite die.

The eccentricities of his younger brother, Richard Waldo Sibthorpe, could hardly have been more different. Instead of a horror of innovation, especially of a mechanical nature, his life was spent in vacillating between the Churches of England and Rome, and in undergoing no less than five conversions from one to the other and back again. As an undergraduate at Magdalen College, Oxford in 1813 he came within an ace of becoming a Catholic, but partly through the efforts of his elder brother the Colonel he was subjected to a stiff course of Anglican apologetics and was meekly ordained into the Church of England. Again to use the words of Sykes, being 'instinctively pious, and naturally mystical, he could not conceivably have followed any profession not ecclesiastical'. By 1835 he had put Rome behind him to such an extent that he was referring to the Vatican as 'Satan's masterpiece'. It should be remembered that Richard was far from alone in the violence of his language. His friend the architect Augustus Welby Pugin, who converted to Rome about this time, felt that there was something quite intolerable about classical or baroque church buildings. On his first visit to the Eternal City, he recorded in his journal that 'the churches here are frightful. St Peter's is far more ugly than I expected, and vilely constructed ... the Vatican a hideous mess, and St Peter's is the greatest failure of all. It is quite painful to walk about.' Pugin's own form of eccentricity took the form of believing quite simply that religion was Gothic, and that Gothic architecture alone was fitting for religious purposes.

Richard Sibthorpe remained a minister in the Anglican Church for twenty-six uneventful years, and was nearly made Vice-President of his college. Instead, he bought a private church at Ryde, in the Isle of Wight, where he built a house and lived in a spacious style, never employing less than six gardeners. But by 1841 dissatisfaction had set in again, and he decided to pay a visit to Bishop Wiseman, the

President of the Catholic Oscott College in Birmingham. When he mentioned to the future Cardinal Newman, still at that time a firm Anglican, 'I am going to Oscott,' Newman replied sharply, 'Mind you don't stop there.' But off Sibthorpe went, and was not only received into the Catholic Church that October, but was ordained a priest seven months later, in his fiftieth year.

But his troubles were only beginning. Instead of the cultivated and gentlemanly circles in which his religious life had been spent for the past thirty years, his work now lay among the uneducated poor in humble homes. The culture shock was too great. The Catholic authorities might well not have allowed him to move, but after a serious carriage accident, and a period of convalescence in Oxford, he was fortunately relieved from parish duties and permitted to move back to the Isle of Wight. He continued to say Mass in an oratory attached to his cottage – until it was gutted by fire. Soon afterwards, for whatever complicated reason, he wrote to inform his old benefactor and friend Dr Routh, still at the age of ninety President of Magdalen, that he had received communion in a parish church, and was returning to the Church of England. Poor Bishop Wiseman, who valued Sibthorpe highly, was so upset by the news that he took to his bed for twenty-four hours, reproaching himself bitterly for having received Sibthorpe into his Church without longer instruction, and for having ordained him so rapidly. He had reason to be sorry. Sibthorpe wrote a letter to an Anglican friend of his called Bickersteth, who could not resist revealing its contents to a Church Missionary meeting in Bath. The conclusion Sibthorpe had reached, he said, was that 'the Church of Rome is the Harlot of Babylon in the Apocalypse. I believe her to be an adulterous and idolatrous church, especially as regards Mariolatry.' But he was not made welcome on his return to the Protestant fold. The Bishop of Winchester, under whose authority he now fell, would only give him permission to become an Anglican minister again on condition that he should live in retirement in Winchester for three years. This not unreasonable ruling might not have given Sibthorpe much trouble had it not coincided with the greatest upheaval in the Church of England for two centuries, namely the secession of Newman to Rome, followed in due course by that of many others. Some years later Disraeli was to describe the departure as 'a blow under which the Establishment still reels'.

Sibthorpe was offended by the reception he received. 'The Church of England,' he said, 'has no bowels of compassion, no feeling, no forgiveness.' But he made a private recantation, was readmitted to Magdalen, and retired to a peaceful existence in his native Lincoln. There he spent a large part of his considerable fortune in building, with Pugin, a suitably gothic collection of Bede-Houses, asylums for the poor, which before the Dissolution had been attached to monasteries and other religious foundations, but many of which had disappeared. Once again, Sibthorpe with his profound spiritual nature should have been happy in a life of prayer and good works. But he was not. He complained of acute boredom in Lincoln; until, that is, he happened to read a life of St John Vianney, the famous Curé d'Ars. Without going into the enormous merits and defects of that heroic figure, it is enough to say that Sibthorpe once again became dissatisfied with the Anglican Communion and at the age of seventy-one was reconciled to the Catholic Church, to the great joy of Cardinal Wiseman. His friend, the Dean of Lincoln, said that 'the news causes me much pain, but no surprise', and his bishop echoed the comment, while paying tribute to Sibthorpe's saintly if changeable character.

For a time Sibthorpe was again happy. He made a little tour of the Catholic shrines and personalities of England, was welcomed by Newman at Birmingham, and attended Manning's consecration as Archbishop of Westminster. He took 350 poor children for an outing in Richmond Park, and then settled in Nottingham, where he had earlier contributed £1,000 to the building of the new Catholic cathedral. At the age of eighty-one, he wrote caustically, as old people do, about the follies and failures of the age. Sometimes he even saw, like his brother the Colonel, now long since dead, enormous dangers where a more level eye saw none. He wrote to a friend: 'I hope your second son will come out of Oxford unscathed. ... Discipline is nearly extinct; cricket, athletics and boating are uppermost. And that vile boat race in London injures very many very seriously.'

But a more serious source of revulsion lay in store. He was, not surprisingly, much upset by the doctrine of papal infallibility. Once again, perhaps echoing the Colonel, or just striking a peculiarly English chord, he notes in his letters the danger of papal authority cutting across national allegiance, much as the threat of Brussels is seen today. Father Sibthorpe loathed the idea of an Italian being able, in theory, to order an Englishman to desist from war in spite of his sovereign's command. But at long last the pendulum had ceased to swing. He died a Catholic in his eighty-seventh year, the Book of Common Prayer in his hand, and it is hard to think of another Catholic priest to have been buried with the full ceremonial of the Church of England. Gladstone described him as a 'truly elect soul', and he remains a more satisfying if enigmatic figure than his brother, if only because his convictions, though shifting, were more seriously and thoughtfully based than the wild flights of the Colonel's fancy. His innate truthfulness – one of the necessary credentials of the true eccentric – explains why he retained the affection of his friends, and it is notable that his various conversions and reconversions never led him anywhere near doubting the validity of Christian revelation.

Although he falls outside the scope of this book, it would be a pity to leave out a man who must have a claim to the ultimate gold medal for religious eccentricity. Rabbi Ovadia Yosef made quite a stir by announcing recently that in his opinion all the victims of the Holocaust fully deserved their fate, since they were merely atoning for grave sins which they had obviously committed in a previous incarnation. Mr Tommy Lapid, the head of a small secular party, who escaped the Nazis as a child, was moved to call the Rabbi, accurately perhaps, 'an old fool'; and he added sharply that 'if the Austrian nationalist leader, Jörg Haider, had said this, we would have declared war on Austria.'

2

Charles Waterton

(1782–1865)

One of the sources of eccentricity undoubtedly lies in a sense of exclusion, rejection and isolation. This is sometimes caused by physical remoteness, and there have always been eccentrics of varying degree in the remoter regions of Northumberland, Lancashire or Dartmoor. But before going on to further individuals, it is worth examining a psychological aspect of eccentricity that also played some part in the case of Father Sibthorpe. For at least two and a half centuries after the curiously inglorious revolution of 1688, Roman Catholics were widely subjected (initially for understandable reasons connected with the far worse treatment meted out to the Protestants in France at the time) to social as well as legal exclusion. This was perhaps particularly noticeable in the group of upper-class families who before the Reformation had owned much property, and held high places in the land, sometimes affectionately known as the Old Catholic Fossils. They had had a lot to lose, and they had lost most of it.

Thanks to the tragic tactlessness and lack of political sense of James II, the fears of the English Protestants were all too real, and the resulting isolation of the English Catholics was correspondingly harsh. They were not allowed to own a horse worth more than £5, on the absurd grounds that it might suddenly become part of an irresistible army of cavalry that would sweep William III off the throne, and all would be to do again. Their isolation was further increased because they were forbidden to sit in Parliament, hold a commission in the army or enter a university.

It would, however, be wrong to generalise. These families were by no means all of them cast down by their deprivations, even those who refused to bend before the storm. From the ranks of such families as the Howards, the Welds, the Throckmortons, the Stourtons, the Stonors, there often emerged individuals of both intellectual and practical distinction, to set against the increasing oddness of some of their innumerable cousins. Many quite simply abandoned the world and became priests and nuns. Others emigrated to more tolerant countries. But the oddities that remained often possessed, and developed, qualities of their own, far removed from success in the eyes of the world but not less remarkable for that.

Of all the great eccentrics of the nineteenth century, none stands out more engagingly than Squire Waterton, of whom Graham Greene observed, rightly or wrongly, that 'Roman Catholicism has always been a great breeder of eccentrics in England. One cannot picture a man like Charles Waterton belonging to any other faith.' Indeed, he was descended on his mother's side from St Thomas More himself; while a Waterton is mentioned by Shakespeare in *Richard II*. By the time Charles Waterton was born in 1782 many of these disabilities had been modified or were no longer much enforced, especially in remoter areas, but the isolation of Catholics still included social ostracism as well as legal restrictions.

All who met Waterton were impressed by the gentleness of his nature and his affection, worthy of St Francis himself, for birds and animals of many kinds. This inspired him, when he inherited the family property at Walton Hall between Leeds and Wakefield, to surround the 300-acre park with a wall, sixteen feet high in places, and to form within it a sanctuary for wild life, in which crows and magpies were made just as welcome as owls and his favourite hedgehogs: 'I am a great friend of the hedgehog,' he wrote. 'On a summer's evening at about four o'clock, you may see my hedgehogs slowly advancing from the woods in quest of food. And if you know how to act, you may approach within two feet of them, and see them thrusting their snouts into the sward, and fetching out fat grubs.'

There was only one exception to this otherwise universal benevolence, but it was a violent one. Waterton's hatred of brown rats was manic. A belief had arisen among Catholics that brown rats were only introduced into England by the Hanoverians, and had overwhelmed the native black rats, with which the Catholics to some extent identified themselves. Waterton would put out an irresistible mixture of porridge and treacle for them, lacing it with arsenic, and watch their deaths with glee. He also had a team of ratting cats, led at one time by a huge Marjay wild cat which he had brought home from the forests of Guyana. (His explorations in South America, amid unspeakable hardships and dangers from predators and poisonous snakes, would fill many chapters.) On one occasion he was said to have caught a rat in his hands, whirled it around by its tail, and dashed its brains out against a wall, with a wild cry of 'Death to all Hanoverians!'

Waterton was nothing if not eccentric. Gerald Durrell, in an introduction to the excellent biography of him by Julia Blackburn (Bodley Head, 1989), said that it read like something invented by Edgar Allan Poe, with a certain amount of help from Richard Jefferies. He once visited Rome, where thanks to his Jesuit connections he obtained an audience with Pope Pius VII, in order to bring him up to date on the religious state of the Indians in South America; but before the audience could take place, he fell in with an old schoolfellow from Stonyhurst, and they decided to climb up to the cross on top of the dome of St Peter's, and to fix their gloves to the lightning conductor, which was thirteen feet higher. This was no undergraduate prank: Waterton was thirty-five. The Pope was not amused, and declining to discuss his South American missions with a couple of English mountebanks, ordered the removal of the gloves. Since no one else was willing to make the ascent, Waterton had to remove them himself. But after many years of tree-climbing, and sometimes tree-dwelling, to observe birds and their nests, he thought nothing of it.

But perhaps the most remarkable of all his adventures in natural history was his feat of capturing a fully grown cayman and riding on its back along a river bank, twisting its forefeet over its shoulders, and being towed along by a team of naked Indians. Fortunately his friend Captain Jones (his companion on the dome of St Peter's, and a competent water-colourist) was at hand, and this unique ride is still preserved on canvas at Stonyhurst.

But as well as his freakishness there was a serious side to Waterton's obsession with natural history, which will greatly endear him to conservationists today. Apart from the bird-protecting activities already mentioned, he was also involved in a series of lawsuits against a soap manufacturer whose works adjoined the Walton Hall estate. The primitive chemical processes that were involved led to the production of quantities of toxic effluent, both liquid and gaseous, which had a devastating effect on the surrounding countryside – and not just over Waterton's own acres. Trees and crops were destroyed far and wide, and human as well as animal health was severely damaged. But all this was hard to lay at the door of the obvious offender, and the manufacturers found it easy to deny liability, even paying witnesses to support their claims to innocence. Though his genuine concern for wildlife was not in doubt, ironically enough Waterton's only tangible success in this field was to have the factory on his boundary removed to another site a few miles off, where, even more ironically, it was considerably expanded and did more damage to the environment than ever – but not on Waterton's doorstep. So, in what is probably the first recorded case of nimbyism, the Squire's feathered friends and their habitats were restored to a flourishing state. Over the years he also recorded extremely thorough and accurate accounts of bird life in the sanctuary that he had created: where and how they nested and brought up their young, and what they preferred to eat.

All his life, Waterton prided himself on his ability to endure violent extremes of physical hardship. After the death of his wife in childbirth, soon after their marriage, he always slept in an attic, where in winter the water in the wash-basin would freeze overnight into a solid block of ice. The window was always open so that owls and bats could come and go as they pleased. He slept on the bare wooden floor, with a wooden pillow and wrapped in an Italian cloak, having 'long learned that a bed is an absolutely useless luxury'. His wardrobe consisted of a stout rope slung across the room, where he would hang the cloak in the daytime, along with a very limited assortment of homespun clothes, and an old apron with a large pocket in front, in which small animals and birds and their eggs could conveniently be stored. It is hardly surprising that one of his friends once described him as looking like 'a spider after a long winter'. On his travels, Julia Blackburn tells us, 'he always took his cloak with him, but he was able to leave the wooden pillow behind, since he had found that his portmanteau served just as well'. At home, he was always up before dawn, and out in the park among his trees and birds. The rain never bothered him, and he would come in dripping like a dog, and then sit on a stool before the drawing-room fire, 'almost lost in the cloud of steam drawn from his clothes by the heat'. His breakfast consisted of a piece of toast and a cup of tea; lunch was bread and watercress, and according to the keeper at the Regent's Park Zoo, when really indulging himself Waterton ate enough 'to sustain a blackbird and two white mice'. Yet outsiders were fascinated by him. One visiting acquaintance found him 'ridiculous and yet immensely dignified', perhaps because he never did anything for effect, but always because for his own strange reasons he thought that his course of action was for the best. Both these characteristics were in evidence when he paid a visit to an orang-utan in the London Zoo and entered its cage. His own description of their encounter could not be bettered:

Nothing struck me more forcibly than the uncommon softness of the inside of his hands. Those of a delicate lady could not have shown a finer texture. He took hold of my wrist and fingered the blue veins therein contained; whilst I myself was lost in admiration at the protuberance of his enormous mouth. He most obligingly let me open it, and thus, I had the best opportunity of examining his two fine rows of teeth.

However odd his habits, Waterton is a wonderful example of how important results may be achieved by following one's principles in the face of the world's derision. He was the first man to warn the Americans of the ultimate danger of destroying their forests, a century or more before it would occur to them themselves. It was Waterton who fought, however vainly, against industrial pollution, who created one of the first nature reserves in the country, and who attacked the destruction of largely harmless birds such as owls, kestrels, ravens and herons, at a time when the damage that they do was magnified out of all proportion by zealous gamekeepers, over intent on impressing their employers by displays of slaughtered vermin. And it was Waterton who benevolently invited inmates of the local lunatic asylum to view his lake and its inhabitants through telescopes from his windows, no doubt to their great benefit. And however extravagant his behaviour may often have been, it did no harm to anyone else, and it suited him throughout a long life. He pestered no one, and made no extravagant claims for his ideas. He is a perfect example of an eccentric who through personal isolation, arising from a variety of causes, showed the way forward in a threatened world.

3

Aubrey and Auberon Herbert

(1880–1923 & 1922–74)

A pair of eccentrics who surprised their friends in a very different way from Waterton, beginning half a century later, were a father and son with confusingly similar names, Aubrey and Auberon Herbert. They were not concerned with natural history, though Aubrey did at one time capture a small shark off the then unknown village of Portofino, on the coast of Liguria, and kept it in a bath until it became a great deal less small, and was somehow released. He also kept a few greater bustards, much hated by his small daughter, whose legs they would peck unmercifully. But his chief priorities lay in what was then called the Near East. At the end of the nineteenth century the Turkish Empire was on its last legs, although its leading politicians were still capable of considerable energy. Some of them became Aubrey's close personal friends.

Aubrey was born into the more intelligent, civilised and politically active reaches of the aristocracy, at a time, so unlike the present, when to be an aristocrat gave one a huge, if unfair, advantage. His father, the Earl of Carnarvon, had been Viceroy of Canada and, very briefly, of Ireland, before resigning in protest against the refusal by the government at home to follow the conciliatory policy that he recommended. Aubrey had a conventional but demanding education at Eton (where in his first term he succeeded in acquiring a jackdaw, a squirrel and a white mouse) and then at Balliol College, Oxford, where, to the surprise of his friends, he won a first class degree in History. Apart from his mercurial nature, what made this truly remarkable was the fact that he had become seriously blind at the age of six, and only regained the sight of one eye after an operation when he was sixteen. This did not, however, prevent him from indulging in the dangerous pastime of climbing over rooftops at night. Twenty years later his friend T.E. Lawrence wrote inviting him to come and stay as his guest at All Souls: '… it's nearly opposite the bank you burgled one night, and that will remind you of several things.' What had in fact happened was that Aubrey had been crossing the rooftops in his usual fashion when he had the misfortune to fall through the roof of the bank, where the manager, who lived on the premises, had held him up at gun point.

After university, he travelled to Japan, by the western route via New York, which he hated, and Canada, which he loved. Falling in with an Oxford friend, he visited a bar where 'we were invited to go upstairs with two Chinese women who looked like diseased telegraph poles'. Having refused the invitation, and unwisely produced a revolver which he was carrying, he admitted that 'the haste with which I left was almost undignified'. He then 'worked' as an honorary attaché at the British Embassy in Tokyo and later in Constantinople.

But all this was symptomatic of a restlessness which never entirely left Aubrey, and which was inherited by his son, another quixotic champion of causes, who admitted modestly that he had always confused movement with action. Probably in both cases it arose in reaction to, or in order to escape from, their mothers' sterner sense of purpose and duty.

Aubrey's next adventure was to set out for the Turkish garrison of Sana'a, a fort in Central Yemen, lately besieged by rebels but eventually relieved by the Turkish general Ahmed Feizi Pasha, who had trekked there, at the age of seventy, from Baghdad, a journey of not less than a thousand miles through the entire length of Arabia. The country was still in a state of armed unrest, but in company with a friend, Leland Buxton, Aubrey sailed down the Red Sea and disembarked at Hodeidah. After pretending to be rich and ignorant big game hunters rather than well-connected but overcurious newshunters, they were not only allowed to proceed into the interior, but were provided with an escort of 150 Turks. After six days' riding (and walking, which Aubrey preferred) through the desert and then the mountains they reached Sana'a, where a population of 70,000 had been reduced to 20,000, and 9000 Ottoman troops had died of starvation in the siege. The Turks, presumably for fear of losing face, had censored all outgoing reports, but Aubrey was now able to send accurate facts and figures to the West for the first time. He and Leland Buxton then set out from Aden to Bombay, though Aubrey was extremely ill with typhoid fever. Once there, Aubrey decided that the Persian Gulf would be a better place for convalescence, and without lingering in India they sailed back to Bahrain, from where they made an abortive attempt to cross the Arabian desert. After making a moonlight flit, on foot, from the fort of Ojain, which was heavily defended against insurgents, Aubrey, still thoroughly weak from typhoid, found that he could go no further, and made his way back to the fort, hoping to re-enter it, as he had left it, by stealth. But he was set on by a savage pack of guard dogs. Aubrey's biographer, his granddaughter Margaret FitzHerbert, has given an account of what followed which could not be bettered:

The noise of the attacking dogs woke the garrison. Aubrey heard a voice shouting from the roof but could pay no attention as he was too busy trying to beat off the dogs. Eventually he drew his revolver and shot one. The others were frightened and withdrew a distance. Meanwhile the great door of the fort opened and soldiers poured out. The Captain greeted him grimly. 'The sentry on the roof has orders to shoot after shouting three times.' he said. 'He disobeyed those orders

tonight; he will be punished tomorrow.' And Suliman, the
Circassian with whom Aubrey had made friends, accompanied
Aubrey to his cell, saying 'Oh my lamb, what wild deeds are
these?'

The next morning Aubrey went to see the Captain to plead the cause
of the imprisoned sentry. The Captain refused to relent, saying he
knew his duty towards all men, guests, enemies or subordinates.
Aubrey replied that he had no desire to instruct him in his duty, but
asked as a favour as one gentleman to another. The Captain replied
'Your pleasure is my will', and the sentry was released. However, the
Captain never forgave Aubrey, and remained stern and unbending for
the remainder of his enforced stay.

Eventually, Aubrey made his way up from Ojain to Baghdad, and
then set out on the 700-mile stretch to Damascus, a well known
endurance test, accompanied by his self-appointed servant Kiazim.
Kiazim was Albanian, and even more unpredictable than Aubrey
himself; Aubrey half-heartedly dismissed him from time to time, but
he had an uncanny capacity for turning up again unexpectedly.
Sometimes he made himself useful, more often he made trouble.
Aubrey was basically devoted to him, but sometimes enough was
enough. With a very different friend, George Lloyd, a school contemporary who was at that time in the embassy in Constantinople,
Aubrey spent Easter in Jerusalem, not an edifying experience. In the
Church of the Holy Sepulchre Aubrey found himself in the middle of
three rival groups, Latins, Greeks and Armenians, who were beating
each other with crosses, sticks and icons. A one-eyed Turkish captain
sent in a few soldiers to break up the fight. When it was over, Aubrey
asked the captain, 'If it is not a rude question, how did you lose your
eye?' The captain replied, 'Ah, that was no honourable wound. I lost
my eye doing what I sent my men to do for you today, preventing
Christians from killing each other.' When he had returned to

26

Constantinople with Lloyd, Aubrey commented shrewdly on the city in an article about his experiences: 'Coveted by the world, it has always been its destiny to bring misfortune to its owners, and itself to be the capital of a dying race, whether Latins, Greeks, Franks or Turks.' Some years later, Kemal Atatürk showed his agreement with this view by moving the capital of the new republic of Turkey to Ankara.

Aubrey was to pay several further visits to Constantinople and Albania between 1907 and 1914, in spite of increasing claims on his presence in England. Having failed twice, in the aftermath of the Liberal landslide of 1906, to be elected as a Conservative candidate for South Somerset, he was successful by a narrow margin in November 1911, and although his subsequent devotion to foreign affairs, which was virtually exclusive, caused frequent complaints among his more domestically-minded constituents, their personal affection for him was undimmed, and he was re-elected until he died. It is hard to imagine a more unconventional Tory, and he once told the whips that he would vote for the party line on Ireland as long as they didn't mind his making a speech in the House of Commons against it.

Nor did another even more important development in his life pin him down geographically. In 1910 he married a rich, beautiful bride, Mary Vesey, almost as headstrong as he was, but with her feet planted more solidly on the ground. Even his deep and real love for her, and his gratitude for her energetic loyalty both on the Somerset estate which he had inherited at Pixton Park, as well as among the often discontented Tories at Yeovil, failed to reduce his determination to follow his star in various corners of the crumbling Ottoman Empire.

But of all his extraordinary feats, none can perhaps compare with Aubrey's determination, in 1914, to join the army, in spite of his very defective eyesight and the many times when he had shown himself more or less unamenable to authority. With the connivance of his wife's cousin, Tom Vesey, a regular soldier in the Irish Guards, he simply called at a military tailor, ordered a uniform of that regiment; and on Wednesday 12 August, when the regiment marched out of Wellington Barracks at 7 a.m. and headed for Nine Elms Station, Aubrey was waiting for them on the pavement. He slipped into their ranks and was later successfully smuggled on board the troopship at Southampton.

On 24 August the Irish Guards were in action in the First Battle of Mons. Never one for regulations, Aubrey kept a forbidden diary that described the attack. They had been sheltering behind a natural earthwork, when

> a really terrific fire opened. It was as if a scythe of bullets passed directly over our heads about a foot above the earthworks. It came in gusts, whistling and sighing ... The turnips seemed to offer some sort of cover, and I thought of the feelings of the partridges, a covey of which rose as we sank ... As we rose, with a number of partridges, the shooting began again, violently but without much effect. Valentine (Castlerosse) was so anxious to reach the trees that he discarded his haversack, scabbard and mackintosh, and for days afterwards walked about with his naked sword as a walking stick.

They then retreated, and 'everybody got very sick of it, and all day long both officers and men were saying how they wanted to turn and fight, though when one was told to do so and realised that we were unchaperoned by the French and faced by about two million Germans, it did something to cool one's pugnacity.'

In the very fierce fighting which followed, Aubrey was hit in the side by a bullet at a range of only fifteen to twenty yards. He was able to get back to his regiment and lie down:

The Red Cross men whistled when they saw my wound, and said the bullet had gone through me. The fire was frightfully hot ... so I asked them to go, as they would only get taken or killed themselves. The doctor gave me some morphia, and I gave them my revolver ... One German motor cyclist, with a bayonet in his hand, was very unpleasant. He said, 'I would like to put this in your throat and turn it round and round.' That sort of thing happened more than once or twice, but there were always more friends than enemies.

Two of his companions from the same railway carriage on the troop train, Lord Castlerosse and Lord Robin Innes-Ker, had also been wounded and taken prisoner, and had unwisely mentioned their titles, hoping to impress their captors. At this point, the French advanced and the Germans had to evacuate the makeshift field hospital. The Germans decided to take these three VIP prisoners with them, who immediately changed their tune. Aubrey, who had told them that he was an MP, said quickly, 'I have only just been elected and have no influence.' 'Mine is a very new creation, I am a nobody,' said Lord Castlerosse, while Innes-Ker, who was a younger son of the Duke of Roxburghe, said, 'Mine is only a courtesy title, I don't count at all.' Luckily for them, the Germans accepted this reassessment of their significance, and they were left behind with the other wounded prisoners.

The French arrived on 11 September, and Aubrey, who had been operated on again to remove the fragmented bullet, and was now in less pain, left the hospital two days later. He was on his way home a month to the day after landing in France. He found that an attitude of nonchalance still prevailed in London, and a general idea that this war, like the Balkan Wars of the two previous years, would be over in a matter of months. Raymond Asquith, one of Aubrey's greatest friends, wrote to congratulate him, saying 'it was thoroughly characteristic of you to be shot and lost but equally characteristic to be found and healed. I would always put my last shilling on your luck in these little things'.

But Aubrey's luck had run out, and far worse was to come for him. Plainly he was unfit for active service, but he seemed an ideal choice for work with the Arab Bureau, set up in Cairo to do whatever it could to destabilise the Turks, who had entered the war largely to protect themselves from Russian designs on Constantinople. By Christmas he was in Cairo, warily and reasonably summing up T.E. Lawrence as 'an odd gnome, half cad, with a touch of genius'. After Mons, he found Cairo 'grotesquely unreal with its Christmas trees and race meetings', but when the disastrous Dardanelles campaign was embarked on, Aubrey was made Liaison Officer and Interpreter to General Godley, the second-in-command of the Anzac Division of Australian and New Zealand troops. He was not to know much about the larger picture of the war, and consequently became violently hostile to Churchill, whose idea the campaign had been. ('I would like to see him die in some of the torments I have seen so many die in here.') He was also outraged by the insouciance of Asquith, whose family were close friends. In one outburst to his wife he wrote that the Prime Minister 'has a mind of granite and the soul of a rather bad bridge party'.

Though not actually fighting, Aubrey was no safer at Anzac Cove than anyone else. Five times he moved his dugout, the previous one having been destroyed by shells. With great difficulty he arranged a truce for the burial of the dead of both sides. He was then sent to Mytilene, a centre of espionage and counter-espionage in which a large role was played by Compton Mackenzie, whose later description of Aubrey was that 'He had of all gallant gentlemen I have met the most endearing personality.' After various attacks of fever he succumbed to dysentery in August and was removed to Alexandria, where his wife, with two friends, had set up a hospital. Colonel

Clayton, the head of the Arab Bureau, asked him to return to London and win over Kitchener and Grey, the Foreign Secretary, to his policy, and decide what inducements should be given to the Arabs in return for their support against the Turks. With singular courage, Aubrey offered to join the force covering the evacuation of Gallipoli which had now been decided on. He pointed out that if he were captured he could, through his endless contacts in Turkish ruling circles, ensure decent treatment for allied prisoners and wounded, and could explore the possibilities of detaching Turkey from the Central Powers. But his offer was admiringly declined on the grounds that it came too late.

Aubrey's own remarkable book about his wartime experiences was rather severely entitled *Mons, Anzac and Kut*. The last of these episodes was even more disastrous and unnecessary, and reflected worse on those responsible, than the second. It arose as follows. In November 1914, the Government of India occupied the town of Basra in Mesopotamia, to protect the oilfields and pipelines of the area from the Turks. By July 1915, the British controlled Lower Mesopotamia, but it was a highly unhealthy region and supplies were short. Consolidation was all that was necessary, but the commander, General Nixon, decided to advance on Baghdad. The Indian Government had promised food, transport, medical supplies and reinforcements. To its eternal shame, none were forthcoming, and the weary and reduced force fell back on Kut.

By the end of April 1916 the starving town had no option but to surrender to their fresh Turkish besiegers, and Aubrey, who was now serving under the Naval Commander-in-Chief Admiral Sir Rosslyn Wemyss was the only Turkish speaker available to negotiate terms. They were not honoured. Many of the large Arab population of Kut were hanged or tortured. Of the British prisoners, who were forced to march the 140-odd kilometres to Baghdad, no less than 70 per cent were to die *en route*. There were incredible stories of meanness

31

and incompetence over the supplies that had been promised by the Indian Government, and Aubrey, strongly supported by Admiral Wemyss, sent an outspoken telegram to Austen Chamberlain, the Secretary of State for War in London. This was strictly against military regulations, and the Government of India pressed the War Office to court-martial Aubrey. The War Office refused. In July, Aubrey, back in London, asked for an inquiry into the conduct of the Mesopotamia campaign. Asquith was evasive, but after four speeches by Aubrey in the House of Commons he yielded, and appointed a Royal Commission, though Hankey, the Cabinet Secretary, complained that he saw no sign in all this of a sincere desire to help the war effort. This may have been so, but what justified Aubrey was the fact that if the guilty men, especially Sir Beauchamp Duff, the Commander-in-Chief, India, and Sir William Meyer, the Financial Secretary, were pursued hard enough, similar horrors were less likely to recur.

Aubrey was now free to concentrate on Albania. The reason for its significance was that back in 1914 Austria had declared war on Serbia, in revenge for the murder of the Archduke Franz Ferdinand at Sarajevo. Serbia, at great cost, had driven the Austrians out, but in the summer of 1915 the Russian front in the Carpathians collapsed, freeing Austrian and German troops to crush Serbia, Russia's unfortunate ally. Great sympathy was felt in Britain for the starving Serbians as they poured through Albania in the hope of escaping through the Adriatic. But if they were to be relieved, a neutral and co-operative Albania was essential. Aubrey had written several memoranda on Albania in November 1915, and his idea that the Italians should be induced to undertake a protectorate of an autonomous Albania was approved by the Foreign Office, who had been responsible for the secret Treaty of London earlier in that year, thanks to which the Italians had entered the war on the allies' side. Aubrey was promoted to Lieutenant-Colonel to increase his standing with the Italians. He failed to persuade them, but kept up a campaign for a free and independent Albania after the war, as will be seen. By early 1918 he was rallying to the support of the admirable but ostracised Lord Lansdowne in his attempt to bring the war to an end without apparently endless further slaughter. Aubrey knew Lansdowne well, but when Lansdowne mentioned his hopes that now that America had entered the war, President Wilson would press for peace, Aubrey retorted memorably that America was a big, fat Cinderella, and that it was 'very rare that a lady who has got her ball-dress and arrived very late at the ball wants it to stop'.

Apart from his support for Lansdowne, April 1918 also saw Aubrey in deep trouble with his own constituency party over the Maurice Debate. General Sir Frederick Maurice had sacrificed his career by writing to *The Times* accusing Lloyd George and Bonar Law of lying to the House of Commons about the strength of the British Army in France. Lloyd George, who had indeed lied, never forgave the ninety-eight Asquith Liberals who voted for an inquiry. They were joined by six pacifist Labour members and a single glorious Unionist in the shape of Aubrey. His local party was furious, and Margot Asquith, in a deranged state of mind, made his position much worse by sending him a telegram at Pixton, urging him to 'Say nothing. Explain nothing. Important letter follows. Asquith.' The local post office did nothing to keep this quiet, and the letter, when it followed, was a dotty pencilled scrawl.

As if all this were not enough, Aubrey was also innocently dragged into an absurd scandal by a dishonest and half-crazed independent MP called Pemberton Billing, who hinted (without foundation) at both immorality and treason on the part of Aubrey and many of his friends in and around the Asquith circle. Fortunately, however, Aubrey was now in charge of something called the British Adriatic Mission, which had been set up by the War Office to report, in co-operation with the Italians, on Austrian and Bulgarian troop movements in Albania and Macedonia. There was also the possibility of raising an Albanian regiment in America, and the US government, which had authorised other ethnic regiments, was in favour. On 17 July the proposal to form the regiment under the command of Colonel Aubrey Herbert was formally approved in Boston 'amid indescribable enthusiasm', according to the official bulletin. The plan was that it should be a unit of the British Army, but the Italians insisted that, even with Aubrey in command, it should nevertheless be part of the Italian Army. The Armistice came before this little local difficulty could be solved.

Aubrey spent the summer of 1918 in the Albanian city of Valona, where the Italian Commander-in-Chief General Ferrero had already organised schools, cleaned up slums and brought order and justice to the area for the first time. Aubrey returned there just at the time when his wife very narrowly escaped from sailing on the Irish mail boat, the *Leinster*, which on the very eve of peace had been sunk by the Germans with the loss of all her passengers, who were of course civilians. However, the Italians, seeing peace imminent, now took up a more imperialist and acquisitive stance over Albania, and Aubrey saw all that he had striven for, with some success, going wrong. He returned to England, in the words of his biographer, 'to find a large overdraft, his friends mostly dead or scattered, and the immediate prospect of a general election in a thoroughly disaffected constituency'. Candidates in the so-called Coupon Election, discreditably spun by Lloyd George, competed with each other in vindictiveness and greed to appeal to the basest emotions of the voters, hardly an atmosphere suited to Aubrey's trustful idealism.

By spring 1919, Aubrey's closest political friends, Alex Thynne and Mark Sykes, were both dead. His first preoccupation was to obtain for the Albanians a fair hearing at the Paris Peace Conference, but needless to say their leaders were buried deep in internal quarrels. Aubrey considered that the Peace Conference was 'run mainly by

Eyre Crowe', an old enemy who was now Permanent Head of the Foreign Office. Aubrey wrote in his diary that 'Wilson was simply bamboozled. Lloyd George does not know what a compass is in morals or in politics. Clemenceau was quite frankly out for revenge, and we got tied to the tail of all this continental hate.' He later also commented in a letter to his uncle Esme Howard, now ambassador in Madrid: 'An accidental truth fell from the lips of Lloyd George when he said that all the world had got shell-shock.' One of his few consolations was to make friends with the Emir Faisal, 'the ablest of the four sons of the Sheriff of Mecca', who later became King of Iraq. Faisal shared Aubrey's contempt for the Peace Conference, and for some reason went up in an aeroplane one day with T.E. Lawrence. Flying over Paris, Faisal remarked 'How dreadful not to have bombs to throw on these people. Never mind, here are some cushions.' And out the cushions went.

Aubrey was much depressed by what he saw as the uncivilised, callous and profiteering atmosphere of England after the war, and especially by the exceptionally low calibre of very many of the new members of the House of Commons, at a time when so many who ought to have been there had been killed. He tried to help form a group of disaffected Conservative members under the leadership of Lord Robert Cecil, a man with a singular reluctance to lead them, and a near-obsession with Anglican ideology in preference to party politics. One of the drawbacks of the group was its almost exclusively aristocratic make-up, including as it did from time to time Lord Henry Cavendish-Bentinck, Edward Wood (later Lord Halifax), Billy Ormsby-Gore (Lord Harlech) and Sam Hoare (Lord Templewood). The youngest was none other than Oswald Mosley, before the time came when he joined the Labour Party and served as a Minister in Ramsay MacDonald's short-lived government. Aubrey wrote with remarkable prescience that 'Mosley has the elements of great success in him, but he will be a lost leader one day.' And in 1922 he commented: 'Tom Mosley is a fox who has lost his tail and wants the rest of us to do the same.' The group had been chiefly held together by hatred and contempt of Lloyd George's licensing of terrorism in Ireland and the operations of the Black and Tans, and also by dislike of the Government's hostility towards Atatürk's nationalist movement in Turkey. Their most positive principle was a faith in the League of Nations, but this was hardly enough to keep a band of such independent idealists together.

At this time the serious possibility arose of Aubrey being offered the throne of Albania. He sought advice from Philip Kerr, who was Lloyd George's Private Secretary until 1921, and who recommended either accepting as a *fait accompli*, or alternatively under Sir Eric Drummond, the Secretary General of the League of Nations. Neither approach appealed to Aubrey, who recorded in his diary that he 'did not want to have the Rupert of Hentzau business' – it was too like D'Annunzio (a poet and megalomaniac who in the turmoil of 1919 had formed an irregular armed force and seized Fiume, in the northeast of Italy, to save it from being incorporated into the new kingdom of Yugoslavia). But he also felt that there was 'more glamour about being a Highland chieftain than Eric Drummond's butler'. After a good deal of hesitation Aubrey in the end came close to accepting some sort of responsibility for the Albanians, though in a form that was never determined. He was however instrumental, with the help of Lord Robert Cecil, in obtaining membership of the League for Albania, and in consequence the assurance of her nationhood. But a good idea of the general situation, possibly biased, though not much so, was given in the comments of Faik Konitza, the brother of the Albanian Foreign Minister, who wrote to Aubrey from America in 1922 that:

the Albanian people has some very fine qualities, and the peasantry has given of late splendid proofs of endurance, patience, love of progress and order. But a gang of crooks, grafters, spies and upstarts has managed to occupy all the leading strategic positions in the body politic and it is more than useless to try and get rid of them. Under such conditions I don't think there is much hope for the salvation of the country.

What Aubrey loved in Albania was open-air travel and adventures in wild country, not the dreary business of trying to sort out stubborn domestic political squabbles in smoke-filled rooms in Paris hotels. Even so, his loyalty to what he regarded as a commitment remained firm.

But something far worse lay in store for Aubrey than these wearisome chores. In the General Election of November 1922 he was again returned with what T.E. Lawrence called 'your usual absurd majority which you would get if you declared yourself a Bolshevik or a Wee Free or a Prohibitionist or a Mormon'. But in the middle of a political speech, darkness had literally descended on him, brought about by the beginning of the detachment of the retina of his right (i.e. good) eye. From then on he could see very little. In July 1923 he attended a gaudy at Balliol, and the next day he was given some fatal advice by his old tutor A.L. Smith, who was himself not only nearly blind, but also suffered from the delusion that there was a close connection between eyesight and teeth. Although also suffering from a duodenal ulcer which his doctor had failed to diagnose, Aubrey had several teeth extracted, possibly following Smith's advice. At any rate, blood poisoning, which was usually fatal until the discovery of antibiotics, set in. He underwent a further operation when the ulcer burst, but died on 23 September.

In the civilised context of Asquith's pre-war government there was at least some scope for public-spirited idealistic MPs who were prepared to concentrate on obscure causes in troubled backwaters, crucial for those directly concerned but utterly remote from the main stream of British political life. By 1919 the atmosphere had totally changed. Aubrey had almost miraculously survived the fate of most of his friends, only to find that the scope for his extraordinary gifts and expertise had melted away. However easy his access had been to the political leaders – Asquith, Grey, Balfour, Curzon and, surprisingly, Bonar Law – they had never seriously backed him, and they had naturally remained preoccupied with the other major European players, France, Germany and even Italy, rather than with the ruins of the Ottoman Empire, on which Aubrey's restless imagination was chiefly concentrated.

When he died, Aubrey was still only forty-three, and his wife Mary was thirty-five. Seventeen months earlier, she had given birth to a son, Auberon Mark Henry Yvo Molyneux Herbert, whose life is an extraordinary echo of his father's. Even in the brave, new post-1945 world of a chilly welfare state, created at a time when England was economically crippled by the war, Auberon's advantages, both social and potentially political, had he chosen to make practical use of them, were enormous, as will be seen. He suffered, of course, from the lack of a father, but if Aubrey had survived, who knows how much he would have been able to help, or discipline, his son? Mary Herbert, in the brief interval between 1923 and 1939, had remained loyal to the cause of Albania, visiting the country every year. Partly under the influence of Hilaire Belloc, an old friend of Aubrey's from Balliol days, she had joined the Catholic Church, and peremptorily sent Auberon to an unsuccessful preparatory school started by Belloc's son-in-law, Reginald Jebb. Auberon later claimed that when the time came for him to move on, he was the only boy left in the school. Impressed by the charismatic figure of the headmaster, Father Paul Nevill, Mary Herbert sent her son on to Ampleforth, where he probably flourished as well as he would have at any public school. His history master in the sixth form later recalled that Auberon was 'obviously able and entirely exasperating, intellectually energetic (perhaps partly thanks to Belloc?) well-read for his age, and entirely disorganised ... other people mattered to him to the almost complete exclusion of self.' Emphasising Auberon's zest for life, and his glorious sense of the ridiculous, his old teacher recalled a memorial in an Oxfordshire churchyard to an eighteenth-century squire who 'by his arrival in the celestial courts, *exhilaravit civitatem Dei*, had an exhilarating effect on the Kingdom of Heaven. So also, I believe, was it with Auberon Herbert.'

At the age of sixteen, he had to give away his youngest sister Laura at her marriage to Evelyn Waugh. Both Auberon and his mother had taken a hearty dislike to Waugh, who in turn considered that the Herberts failed to play the part of conventional minor aristocrats and substantial landowners in a manner of which he, from his more modest background, could approve. It was said that on their way to the church Auberon begged his sister with tears in his eyes to back out of the marriage while there was still time; but not surprisingly she chose to stick to her bridegroom, whatever his personal drawbacks, rather than to her tearful schoolboy brother.

After leaving Ampleforth in 1939 Auberon did his best to join the army, but the cavalier method followed by his father in 1914 was no longer an option. Apart from that, he suffered from a sort of counterpart of his father's blindness: the after effects of a serious operation for double mastoid, which left him slightly disfigured for life, combined with a large pair of flat feet, made his rejection inevitable. He spent two years in wartime Oxford, where he followed his father to Balliol – but a very different Balliol from that of 1900 – and was at one time sent down for pushing his landlady down the stairs (his defence, that she had insulted his religion through the keyhole of the bathroom door, not being accepted). After vainly trying the Free French, and even the Dutch Resistance, he reflected that the war had been triggered off by Hitler's invasion of Poland. Consequently, he decided that it would be the most natural thing in the world to join the Polish Army, then training under General Anders in the Borders of Scotland. After injuring his leg in the course of parachute training, he was transferred to the Polish 1st Armoured Division, as the only British officer in the Polish Army, an echo of his father's nomination as commander of the Albanian Regiment from America. He fought his way through Belgium and Holland in the winter of 1944, and was then entrusted with a mission to Anders from Winston Churchill, his father's old sparring partner from the days of Gallipoli. But in his accident-prone fashion, Auberon fell out with members of the Canadian Military Police in Ghent, having become temporarily separated from his military identity papers. This, combined with his archaic habit of speech, and the considerable amount of hard cash in his pockets, convinced them that he was a spy. Before he could eventually establish his exalted credentials, he was beaten up by the Canadians to an extent which left his face scarred for life.

When the war was over, Auberon devoted his energies and much of his resources to the cause of his Polish comrades in arms, especially those who decided, often in a somewhat prickly fashion, to make a new life for themselves in Britain. Auberon felt that Poland had been shamefully betrayed to Stalin, which was largely true, though it must be remembered that Churchill had sadly few cards to play at the Yalta Conference, and Roosevelt, who was a dying man, washed his hands of Eastern Europe. The Russians were already in Poland, having murdered thousands of Polish officers in the Katyn Woods, and were ruthlessly persecuting the Catholic Church, of which Auberon was such a staunch member. His sense of personal honour and obligation inspired him to throw himself with great generosity into the work of the Polish Resettlement Corps, which did what it could to smooth the way of those Poles who had accepted the offer of settling in Britain. Auberon was able to find jobs and homes for quite a number of them, as well as helping the morale of many others; and he thus contributed more directly to their welfare than his father had done for the Albanians after 1918. He was later awarded the civil decoration Polonia Restituta, in a form rarely given to foreigners.

When in due course the Poles had largely found their feet, Auberon turned his attention to their neighbours from Ukraine and Byelorussia, even though many of them had not been our allies in the war. They also lacked the panache and wayward charm of many of the Poles, but for Auberon they were the victims of hateful Communist oppression and consequently had an automatic claim on his benevolence.

His attempts to be adopted for a winnable seat in Parliament were unsuccessful, though at Aberavon he endeared himself locally by adding a smattering of Welsh to his already impressive list of languages, and also by learning to propel a coracle on the local river. Later, at Sunderland, he came much nearer to success, but his lack of discipline, whether in party policy or personal habits, always told against him in the eyes of selection committees. This was in spite of his warm friendships with the new generation of several of Aubrey's old friends such as the Macmillans, Amerys and Ormsby-Gores. Auberon chose to believe that his failure to be adopted for the safe seat of Taunton, next to his father's old constituency, was due to anti-Catholic prejudice in an area then containing a substantial non-Conformist vote. There may have been an element of truth in this, but the fact was that the selectors preferred someone less unconventional, more reliable, and above all readier to take a regular interest in the topics which affected most people's daily lives. Yet several leading politicians, even if they could not include him in their fold, nevertheless loved him for his transparent integrity, his generosity of spirit, his keen sense of humour and his even keener sense of honour in an increasingly shabby political atmosphere. And he found the time to go on dreaming what appeared to be impossible dreams about ending the nightmare tyranny of the Soviet Empire. It was an added irony that the first cracks in its structure should arise, after Auberon's death, through the undaunted efforts of his beloved Poles, and above all that a Polish pope should come to play such a crucial, and quite unforeseen, role in the demolition of the Iron Curtain. However weird his priorities often seemed to his contemporaries, his thinking was in fact a mere twenty years ahead of its time. Nor did he entirely neglect matters nearer home. He found opportunities for idiosyncratic action on various local councils in Somerset, as when he urged, with *Lorna Doone* in mind, that the public lavatories in the Exmoor National Park should be labelled Lorna and Jan rather Ladies and Gentlemen. In the rather infertile expanse of the Pixton estate, his thoughts turned, sensibly, to forestry. Here again his approach was idiosyncratic, not least in the planting of a wood called Britannia's Shield, where the colour scheme of the trees was the first priority. It formed a wood of about five acres, on the basis of the Union Jack: red was American Oak, white was acacia, and blue was silver spruce.

No account of Auberon would be complete without mentioning his sometimes copious intake of alcohol. It is usually difficult to guess at the causes for this habit, but in his case it was developed amid the severe worries and frustrations which plagued the Polish forces in which he served as a very young man. The result was not helpful to self-discipline but in a book of tributes to him written by a number of his more distinguished friends, including Patrick Leigh Fermor and Malcolm Muggeridge, and published soon after his death, Sir Isaiah Berlin recalled that 'Auberon's manners were impeccable, whether he was tipsy or sober … he was sometimes monotonous and glazed, never embarrassing … His faith, which was deep, childlike, beset by no genuine doubts, and the supreme value of his life, preserved him and kept him from ultimate despair. He was, above all, an extraordinarily good man, and this shone through everything he did …' Although Auberon spent far less time in the corridors of power than his father had quite easily been able to do, it is arguable that through his personal generosity and spontaneous fellow feeling with many individuals in need of a boost, his achievement, though different, was by no means inferior.

Before leaving the political scene it is worth noticing that eccentricity can be infectious, and that a whole group of individuals can catch it from each other in pursuit of a cause. The fact that the cause may be unreasonable or absurd in the highest degree makes not the slightest difference. Take, for example, the Socialist Party of Great Britain, a faction very far removed from the quixotic ways of the Herberts, although both father and son, each in his own unpredictable way, might easily have made friends with its individual members and felt a certain wild sympathy with the Party's truly eccentric and bewilderingly rigid views. There could be no more eloquent description of them than that by Bernard Levin; his words, unlike those of most journalists, were far too well chosen to be paraphrased:

The Socialist Party of Great Britain was originally a fragment of the cosmic dust resulting from the 'big bang' of Marxism in the nineteenth century. The proliferation of socialist, utopian sects around the end of Victoria's reign was largely the result of the passionate intensity with which almost every individual in them maintained that there was but the one true faith and that he alone held it. The SPGB originated from a group expelled from Hyndman's Social Democratic Federation for some inconceivably obscure variety of deviationism, and is unique not just in that it is the most extreme of all Impossibilist sects, but because it has remained absolutely unchanged in its beliefs from 1904 to the present day.

The original declaration of aims stated that the SPGB was 'hostile to every other party', and that it was determined to wage war against all other political parties, whether allegedly labour or avowedly capitalist. And to this position it has adhered ever since, with absolutely literal fidelity; it is perfectly fair to say that its members believe that there is *nothing what-soever* to choose between the Labour Party and the National Front, or between the Communist Party and the Tories.

The SPGB's position is simple, and has always been. Marx was right; and the SPGB's interpretation of Marx is right; there is no possibility at all of anything happening to improve the lot of the people until, overnight, they seize control of their own destiny and enact Socialism; none but the SPGB can convert them to that view. It follows that all attempts at reform of any kind must be implacably resisted, partly because they are all devised by the capitalist class to further their own ends, and partly because they delay the dawn.

Thus, its members are immovably opposed to the Welfare State; they have opposed the introduction of holidays with pay because these only refresh the workers for more exploited labour; when they put up candidates for local councils or for Parliament (and they have always been very dubious about doing so) they spend much of their electioneering time insisting that only voters who are one hundred per cent supporters of everything they stand for may vote for them; they fought against the introduction of safeguards for factory machinery because it might put off the day when the downtrodden (and, presumably, mutilated) workers take over the means of production, distribution and change; they refused to accept advertising in their paper (the *Socialist Standard*) though they have always been desperately poor, because advertising is a filthy capitalist habit, despite the fact that at the time they took the decision they had only ever had one advertiser, and that he was the Party member who printed the Party Journal at ruinous cost to his little printing business, which he wanted to see survive solely so that he could go on producing it for his comrades; and one member, hardly exceptional among his fellows, 'would have no furniture because, he said, capitalists sent bailiffs to take such things away from working people, and so his family used orange boxes instead.'

It is not difficult to guess what this Impossibilism has led to, again and again, throughout the Party's history: a succession of atrocious purges and heresy hunts, of a medieval intolerance and ferocity, within the ranks of the Elect. Again and again, their best men have been thrown out for daring to suggest the tiniest variation in the interpretation of Holy Writ; whole branches (sometimes amounting to a substantial proportion of the whole membership, which has rarely been more than a few hundred) have been expelled; and every time there was a vote on an expulsion, those who have voted against it were themselves forthwith expelled, followed by any who had voted against *their* expulsion.

Until very recent times, the SPGB's story has been largely composed of some marvellously colourful figures; there was Moses Baritz, for instance, who, barred from a meeting of a rival organisation, 'climbed onto the roof with a clarinet, and blew piercing, unbearable *obbligatos* into the hall until they let him in.' And there was Tony Turner, who I heard speak many times, and who was certainly the greatest soap-box orator I can remember (he once spoke, in Hyde Park, from early morning till late at night, without a break).

The author of the history of the movement, one Robert Barltopp, is himself a lifelong member, though he left the Party for some years, and may well be expelled for heresy because of this book; it is written with an honesty that is beautiful to contemplate, a self-taught style of extraordinary grace, and –

Anathema sit! *Anathema sit*! – considerable humour. He tells a tale of gorgeous absurdity: of a Party which expelled a member for turning up at a meeting, during the Second World War, with his gas mask, because the Party had ruled that the war was about nothing but capitalist rivalry; a Party with a faction that argued that 'vegetarianism was a capitalist plot to lower labour costs by making the working-class feed on grass'; a Party which, facing financial extinction, was saved by a large donation from a 92-year-old sympathiser with a cat called Karl Marx; a Party which has survived for seventy-two years by an implacable refusal to recognise any form of reality. I hope it goes on refusing for another seventy-two years at least, for when it dies England will have lost a monument indeed.

These words were written thirty years ago, but happily the Party *does* still survive, at the rather good address of 52, Clapham High Street.

4

John Christie of Glyndebourne

(1882–1962)

Of all the English eccentrics of the twentieth century, none can have had a more far-reaching or impressive effect on the cultural scene than John Christie of Glyndebourne, although his family contained a streak of eccentricity so extreme that his father's last will (leaving a large family property in Devon to a distant cousin) was set aside, after a lawsuit involving the best known counsel in England on both sides, on the grounds of insanity.

John Christie was very far from insane. Born in 1882, he was the only child of a deeply unhappy marriage, and his early life was a lonely turmoil which must almost certainly have increased any latent, innate eccentricity. He became fascinated by scientific experiments while still at Eton, at a time when teaching of the subject was rudimentary. (It is true to say that Christie's teacher, one Dr T.C. Porter, was no mean eccentric himself. At the end of the term he would give what he called 'good boy lectures', preceded by an enormous tea, and including such delights as a home-made volcano. They always contained a thrilling element of danger, and according to Christie's biographer 'casualties were not unknown'. But by 1930 no fewer than six of his former pupils were Fellows of the Royal Society.)

Christie read science at Cambridge, and returned to teach it at Eton in 1906 for no less than sixteen years. But he had already shown an interest in opera as well as in engineering. In the summer of 1904 he had set off with three friends, including the Head of Music at Eton, Dr Lloyd, on what his biographer has called 'an audacious expedition' to Bayreuth, in an early, and much adapted, two-seater car. To accommodate the passengers, luggage, and many cans of petrol and spare tyres, Christie acquired a strange vehicle, originally designed for the transport of cheese, and nailed it to the back of his car. The party reached Dover successfully, only to discover that the cross-channel steamers had no equipment for taking cars on board. Glancing round the harbour, Christie spied an unoccupied barge moored beside a pier. He immediately chartered it, loaded up the car and its passengers, and was safely towed across the channel behind the steamer.

By 1914 he had lost the sight of one eye through being hit by a racket ball, and had badly damaged a knee falling from a horse. But he passed the army medical examination by what he called 'a dodge' (a favourite expression) and suffered through the worst of the battle of Ypres, writing nonchalantly to his uncle from the trenches, 'I hope I don't get any gas. I don't much mind the idea of bullets, they are so small.' At one stage, while under heavy fire, he produced a copy of Spenser's *The Faerie Queene* from his pocket, as if he had been in a classroom, and read it to his men as an improbable aid to morale, while the shells burst around them.

After two years, the military authorities finally discovered his precarious physical condition, and he returned to his teaching job at Eton. But it was not enough. And on inheriting the Glyndebourne estate, he decided that the only justification of land ownership was to accept a moral obligation to develop practical undertakings on the estate, and to provide as many as possible of the jobs which were so much needed after the war. Growing and selling timber, garages, waterworks, hotels, house-building, golf courses, all at one time or another occupied his attention, and he despised landowners who failed to give a lead in this way, perhaps a shade unfairly, since through the sale of outlying property his own capital base was a good deal more secure than that of others. Later, he was to show the same single-minded determination in the establishment of opera at Glyndebourne, though if he had not married a professional singer with personal experience of life in rehearsal and on stage, it is very doubtful that the project would have succeeded. Audrey Mildmay was a wife in a million. Apart from her professional expertise, she was possessed of tact, thoughtfulness for others and common sense to a remarkable degree, and somehow managed to be at the same time a singer of great charm as well as an inspired hostess.

Not surprisingly, the technical side of the opera was the one where Christie was most at home. The design and regular adjustment of the theatre and its contents was one of his chief specialities. But none of this would have been enough without his passionate determination to appoint musicians and directors of the highest international standard. By a well-deserved stroke of luck for Glyndebourne, two great Germans, the producer Carl Ebert and the conductor Fritz Busch, though not themselves Jewish, decided in 1933 that they were no longer willing to work in a Germany dominated by Hitler. Their services were therefore available, and after considerable initial misgivings they recognised Christie's craving for excellence, and were delighted by both the idyllic surroundings of the theatre, and by the Christies' personal charm and seriousness about the project. 'Do the best you can,' Christie told Ebert, 'because I want to give my country a model of perfection.'

The seasons of 1934-9 were a triumphant success with audiences and critics alike, even those who initially scoffed at the idea of 'Mozart in a hayfield', and who, not surprisingly, found it tedious to change into evening dress after lunch in order to take the train from London to Lewes in time for the performance. Yet in this too there was a weird logic behind Christie's demands. His view was that an enormous amount of trouble was taken by the musicians, and it was up to the audiences to recognise this and show respect for it by taking a modicum of trouble themselves. His rule is observed, more or less, to this day.

When war came, and the opera disappeared for six years, it sometimes seemed unlikely that Glyndebourne could be revived. But a formula was found, first through putting on productions at the Edinburgh Festival, and later through a very successful scheme of individual and corporate sponsorship, and by the mid-fifties Glyndebourne was once more in full swing. Very typical of Christie's indifference to what he didn't consider important was the fact that when the Queen and Princess Margaret came to Glyndebourne in 1958, he didn't bother to tell Ebert until shortly before he and the company were presented to her after the performance. Ultimately, what made his eccentric approach work was his single-mindedness, his inherited wealth, carefully used (he spent a lot of time going round the theatre turning lights out after the performances) and his physical energy (a stage manager observed that 'when there was anything to be moved, Mr Christie always took the heavy end'). There was also his obstinacy, his gift for appointing a brilliant team of experts, a fair measure of luck, above all when he fell in love with a uniquely and indispensably well-qualified wife. He was indifferent to the possibility of making enemies, and his contempt for the standards of Covent Garden was loudly and frequently expressed. This, among other things, gained him the hostility of his near neighbour in Sussex, John Maynard Keynes, the founder of the Arts Council, and they refrained from speaking to each other on Lewes station, which they both used for travelling to London. Christie could not have cared less, and was always determined not to seek a penny of public money for Glyndebourne.

The world of opera, not just in England, is everlastingly and deeply indebted to his unfailing and unbounded optimism, and to his truly remarkable ability to reconcile the ideal with the practical. His son, now Sir George, though hardly his equal in eccentricity, has shown an extraordinary ingenuity and single-mindedness (not to mention diplomatic skills which were of no interest to his father): the best example of this is his achievement with his team of advisers in raising no less than £32m in order to pull down the original opera house, which was on its last legs, and rebuild it, half as big again as the original. Almost more remarkably, the job was completed on time and within budget.

5

William Beckford

(1759–1844)

Going back a century, but remaining in the field of music and building, it is worth considering a figure as different as possible from John Christie. William Beckford's life is perhaps more fully documented and written about than that of any other great English Eccentrics. He achieved more in the way of building and collecting than any of his contemporaries, even though most of what he built or collected has vanished or been dispersed, with the exception of his Tower on Lansdowne Hill, on the edge of Bath, and some of the inheritance of his daughter the Duchess of Hamilton.

Beckford's father was an immensely rich owner of plantations in Jamaica, an alderman and twice Lord Mayor of London, who in spite of rough and uncouth manners was a notable collector and the builder of a magnificent house, Fonthill Splendens, on the estate that he bought in Wiltshire in 1734. But he was not a parvenu. The family fortune had been formed by Beckford's great-grandfather Peter Beckford, who died fifty years before William was born. William's godfather was no less a figure than William Pitt, Earl of Chatham, who died when William was only ten. William inherited not only the family fortune but also 'wilfulness, petulance and an unbridled temper', though none of the masculinity which had provided him with at least six illegitimate half-brothers, and according to Horace Walpole, many more. At the age of five William was given music lessons by the eight-year-old prodigy Mozart, who he later referred to haughtily as 'that moonstruck, wayward boy'. Later he attended performances of all Mozart's operas in London, score in hand, loudly hissing when singers or players made a mistake. His vanity was such that he even claimed the aria *Non piu andrai* in the *Marriage of Figaro* as his own composition.

Fonthill Splendens contained a vast Egyptian hall, eighty-five feet long, and a much smaller but equally exotic Turkish Room, enlarged by mirrors on the window shutters, and crowned with a coved ceiling painted with arabesques and flowers on a gold ground, soon to be an important part of the inspiration for Beckford's first literary venture. To teach him drawing, his mother engaged the romantic artist Alexander Cozens, who also regaled him with tales of the glamour of St Petersburg (where Cozens was born) and introduced him to the magical world of the *Arabian Nights*. Too late, Mrs Beckford tried to divert William from all these fancies, first by sending him at the age of seventeen to finish his education in Geneva, where he not only met Voltaire but quickly mastered Spanish, Portuguese, Italian, and German; and secondly by sending him, along with a tutor, on a tour of English country houses, where she hoped that he would pick up some conventional English country tastes.

His hatred of all blood sports was already well advanced, and one of his life's many ironies was the fact that in 1840 his Fonthill estate was acquired by the Morrison family from Glasgow, and was occupied for the second half of the twentieth century by John Morrison, first Lord Margadale, one of the best shots of his day and Master of the South & West Wilts hounds for many years, but a man with no interest in the arts. Beckford loved galloping about the Fonthill estate, adored animals and established such a rapport with them that hares would come and eat out of his hand.

On his tour of country houses at the age of nineteen, Beckford fell disastrously in love with the eleven-year-old heir of Powderham Castle and future Earl of Devon, William Courtenay. With a fatal mixture of euphoria and hubris, he made no secret of his infatuation in either the Beckford or Courtenay household. At about the same time his mother, again misguidedly as it turned out, invited to Fonthill her husband's nephew Peter Beckford, the future author of one of the most famous books of its kind, *Thoughts on Hunting*. Not only did this utterly fail to kindle in William any enthusiasm for the chase, but Peter Beckford's young wife Louisa fell violently in love with William and agreed to act as an accomplice in his relations with Courtenay.

However, neither of these passions prevented William from marrying in May 1783 the pretty, charming twenty-year-old Lady Margaret Gordon, who became easily the most attractive figure in Beckford's tangled story. She was full of kindness and concern for her husband, in spite of his sexual duplicity, and after her death only three years later, Beckford worshipped her memory throughout his fifty-eight years as a widower. However, the scandal over Courtenay soon became public, and although William was never prosecuted for what was then a capital offence, his name was blackened, and disastrously for his character he was ostracised from a society in which his vast wealth and his passion for music and the arts could have made him an outstanding figure. Instead, with occasional striking exceptions, he became, in the words of one of his two best biographers, James Lees-Milne, 'increasingly embittered, ruthless and cruel ... as well as solitary and introspective', and more and more deeply and selfishly immersed in his own aesthetic appetites. Typically, he broke with Courtenay, whose life he had done so much to ruin, and who fled the country in 1811, never to return.

Before going on to Beckford's merits as a writer, which became considerable, and his talents as a collector and builder, which were patchy, it is worth pointing out that his personal character was full of unattractive contradictions. He genuinely hated the minor cruelty of hunting and fishing, but chose to ignore the plain fact that animals are often far crueller to each other than human beings are to them.

He revelled, kinkily, in macabre and sadistic literature. There are already sadistic elements in *Vathek*, which he wrote at the age of twenty-two – an astonishing tour de force, probably inspired by the celebrations for his coming of age, in the exotic surroundings of Fonthill Splendens already mentioned. He refused to support the anti-slavery movement, and in all his long life never took the faintest interest in the lives of the negro slaves on the property in Jamaica which provided him with the vast resources which he was able to devote to building and collecting. Yet he did protest loudly at the condition of agricultural labourers in Wiltshire under the govern-ment of Pitt, who he no doubt considered his enemy after their childhood friendship. And although he paid inflated wages to the builders at Fonthill, they spent most of them on drink, sometimes destroying their health, and also accelerating the collapse of the building itself. In a bad winter, it is true, he distributed hundreds of blankets, and generous supplies of coal to estate workers; and when he sold Fonthill he gave twenty acres of land to the poor of the neigh-bouring village of Hindon, on which to grow vegetables. But these were capricious, one-off hand-outs, to satisfy a passing whim: never was there any steady continuity in his benevolence towards humans; it was only the Wiltshire foxes that enjoyed his lasting protection. According to Lees-Milne, he had 'a strong inclination to Christianity, but no religious faith, except for an intermittent dread of eternal punishment'. He saw the validity of the Catholic Church, but never came anywhere near to accepting its disciplines. He loathed the Church of England, but apparently on eccentric aesthetic grounds of his own, which can hardly have been shared by anyone else before or since. In 1808 he wrote to his factotum, Gregorio Franchi, on the subject of Salisbury Cathedral, as follows:

I've always found the said Cathedral poor, bare and insipid, without mystery, without ecclesiastical pomp; only the tower is any good. Wyatt's work there is infamous. Oh the disgust and stink of Protestantism (it doesn't deserve the sonorous name of Heresy). All these windows, all this light, all this glass with its small diamond-shaped panes make this shameless church look like a whore clad only in muslin – what an infamous spot. How I abhor it.

He didn't like Westminster Abbey either:

If the building was purged by celestial Catholic fire of all the foulness of infamous Protestantism it would be capable of producing the most majestic effect imaginable ...

The exterior of Salisbury was quite a different matter, and it was that which gave Beckford his inspiration for the vast Gothic extravaganza of Fonthill Abbey, the building for which he remains best known, even though its execution was disastrous, largely thanks to his childish impatience. The result was a jerry-built pile, made of the shoddiest materials, put up by inexperienced and often drunken workmen, who were kept on the job round the clock. This is under-standable when one remembers that all Beckford was principally interested in was creating theatrical effects, partly in revenge for the social snubs inflicted by his neighbours, and generally to put them in the shade. As he put it, 'Some people drink to forget their unhappiness. I do not drink. I build.' His choice of architect did not help. James Wyatt had many qualities, but reliability was emphatically not one of them, and this, combined with Beckford's frequent absences and indecisions, led to many rows. Spurred into action by finding a pack of hounds trespassing on his land, he immediately gave orders for a seven-foot wall to be built, twelve feet high, round the inner domain, to keep out hounds and any other unwanted trespassers.

Work began on the Abbey in October 1796, and though much of

the tower came crashing down in a gale in the following spring, Fonthill Splendens was still intact, and there Beckford brought off one of his few social coups by entertaining Nelson in the course of a triumphant tour of the West of England. This was due to Nelson's passion for Emma Hamilton, whose complaisant husband was related to Beckford. Innumerable plans and prints of the Abbey have survived and are easily accessible to those interested, so this is not the place to go into details. It is enough to say that Beckford, who was never satisfied with anything for long, later admitted that the composition was faulty, there was a want of balance, and 'disproportion prevails in every part of the exterior'. And as a place to live, it had every conceivable disadvantage. Yet for dyed-in-the-wool lovers of the Romantic, the building was beyond compare. And Beckford's modest claim that 'the Abbey cannot be contemplated without emotions that have never been excited by any building erected by any private individual in our times', can certainly not be denied.

Yet if his selfishness and other failings were repulsive there was much to his credit. His work with the pen is hard to fault. The descriptions in his *Journal in Portugal and Spain 1787-1788* read as freshly and delightfully today as when they were written. He was made welcome in the highest circles in Lisbon, where the atmosphere was very much to his taste. As Lees-Milne has put it, it was 'a kind of Alice in Wonderland world, where nothing is unexpected, where marquesas and dwarfs, mitred abbots and peasants dance an eternal fandango of high spirits and silliness'. On one occasion he was taken by his great friend and constant host the Marquis of Marialva on a visit to the descendants, literally, of the Holy Crows which had torn out the eyes of the murderers of St Vincent, patron saint of Lisbon Cathedral. He described it as follows:

> When we entered this gloomy edifice, the crows, I believe, had gone quietly to roost, but a sacristan officiously roused them.

Oh how sleek and plump and glossy they are! My admiration of their size, their plumage and their deep-toned croakings carried me, I fear, beyond the bounds of saintly decorum. I was just stretching out my hands to stroke their feathers when the Marquis checked me with a solemn, reproachful look ... while the sacristan and an old toothless priest, almost bent double, communicated a long string of anecdotes concerning these present Holy Crows, their immediate predecessors, and other crows in the old time. ... The Marquis listened with implicit faith and attention, never opening his lips during the half hour we remained, except to enforce our veneration and to exclaim with the most pious composure, *Honorado Corvo*!

Beckford had attached to him at this time a young Italian musician called Gregorio Franchi, who returned with him to Fonthill. The Wiltshire neighbours referred to him as 'the Portugal orange' and he became the subject of unmerited gossip and scandalous hints which were in fact unfounded. But for thirty years Franchi devoted himself to Beckford's service, running errands for him, buying books and treasures of all kinds for him; always good-humoured, constantly patching up quarrels between the servants and even interceding successfully with the proud Duke of Hamilton, Beckford's son-in-law. Yet in 1818 poor Franchi became crippled with gout and arthritis, and died in great poverty and distress in a London lodging house while Beckford was closeted in the comforts of Lansdowne Crescent in Bath, where he had retired after having sold the dilapidated remains of Fonthill. Nothing could be more unattractive about Beckford than this infinitely cruel neglect of someone who he had dearly loved and who had done everything possible to serve him not as a mere secretary but in Lees-Milne's words as 'the best friend he ever had. And the reason? Simply that the Caliph of Fonthill could not bear unpleasantness of any sort'.

To return, with some difficulty, to the credit side: as well as his literary gifts Beckford was a collector of genius. It would take many pages to give a proper idea of the pictures and furniture that he amassed. Today, the National Gallery contains no fewer than twenty paintings formerly bought by Beckford, including the famous Raphael of 'St Catherine of Alexandria', Giovanni Bellini's equally famous portrait of 'Doge Leonardo Loredan', Elsheimer's 'Tobias and the Angel', a 'Holy Family' by Garofalo, and sacred paintings in the style of Orcagna and Van der Weyden. Other masterpieces that he owned from time to time are also to be found in the Frick and the Metropolitan Museums in New York, the Thyssen Collection and the Berlin Museum, among others. He was often ahead of the fashion. When an artist became too popular, he would sell what he had bought, usually at a good profit. (In 1808 Beckford sold for 12,000 guineas the Altieri Claudes, now at Anglesey Abbey, for which he had paid 6,500 nine years earlier.) And twenty years before, at the height of the French Revolution, he had descended on Paris like a vulture, snapping up treasures while their owners were led off to the guillotine. He acquired the outstanding 'Van Dieman' seventeenth-century black lacquer box, inlaid in gold and silver with scenes of Japanese court life, now in the Victoria & Albert Museum, and formerly owned by Madame de Pompadour. He also bought at that time a roll-top desk by Riesener, now in the Wallace Collection, but made for King Stanislas of Poland. Although his life was in danger after France declared war on England in 1793, he never lacked courage; he remained in Paris, and worked, disguised as an assistant, in a famous bookshop, Merigot's. One could easily go on. By the time Beckford moved to Bath, the great connoisseur and art historian G.F. Waagen rated the dining-room in his house in Lansdowne Crescent as 'taken all in all, perhaps one of the most beautiful in the world'.

As with paintings, furniture and *objets d'art*, so with books. By the time he sold Fonthill, Beckford owned no fewer than 800 illuminated manuscripts ranging from the ninth century to the sixteenth. Even before the French Revolution he was buying the rarest and grandest books, outbidding the King of France at the Duc de la Vallière's sale in 1784. On the whole he avoided sales at which the highest prices were to be expected, such as the Duke of Roxburghe's in 1812, but picked up many a bargain when the Duke of Marlborough suddenly went bankrupt in 1819, acquiring a valuable Froissart manuscript for £32 'when the Persian Ambassador, in exotic robes, passed the auctioneer's window and most of the buyers rushed to have a look at him'. And unlike many collectors, Beckford was an omnivorous reader, seldom if ever buying a book that he did not read. On his death in 1844, his library, in spite of the frequent sale of books for which he had no longer space, was valued at £30,000. His daughter, the Duchess of Hamilton, would not have her father's books sold, but when her grandson included them in the Hamilton Palace sale in 1882, they fetched the enormous sum of £73,551.18s. The range of subject matter was very wide: Greek and Latin classics, architecture, travel, engravings of paintings, theology, European literature, contemporary English poetry, and the bizarre. But as in other matters, Beckford was easily displeased by anything he considered pretentious or silly. In a book of memoirs, he scribbled the words 'Those who like Hog-Wash, and there are amateurs for everything, will not turn away disgusted or disappointed with this book, but relish the stale, trashy anecdotes it contains, and gobble them up with avidity.' And like many others, he grew more caustic with old age. In his copy of Mary Shelley's *Frankenstein*, which he might have been expected to have enjoyed, he wrote 'This is, perhaps, the foulest toadstool that has yet sprung up from the reeking dunghill of the present times.' And however much his judgement differed from that of others, there is a splendid integrity in his vitriolic dismissal of Gibbon:

The time is not far distant, Mr Gibbon, when your almost ludicrous self-complacency, your numerous, and sometimes apparently wilful mistakes, your frequent distortions of historical Truth to provoke a jibe, or excite a sneer at everything most sacred and venerable, your ignorance of the oriental languages, your limited and far from acutely critical knowledge of the Latin and Greek, and in the midst of all the prurient and obscene gossip of your notes ... your heartless scepticism, your unclassical fondness for meretricious ornament, your tumid diction, your monotonous jingle of periods, will be still more exposed and scouted than they have been. Once kicked off from your lofty, bedizened stilts, you will be reduced to your just level and true standard.

Gibbon was highly sensitive about his dwarfish body, so the reference to stilts is hardly generous, but anyone who looks at the notes in Dean Milman's edition of *The Decline and Fall of the Roman Empire*, will see that there is much truth in Beckford's complaint about inaccuracies, and that whatever his merits, automatic veneration is not an appropriate reaction to Gibbon.

Beckford also took the greatest care of his books, in a way in which eccentricity bordered on perfectionism. All the books in his library were protected from direct sunlight. No gas lighting was allowed, the rooms were not lit by oil lamps, or even entered after dark, and the temperature and dryness of the air were strictly controlled.

By the 1820s his financial situation, in spite of an income that at one time reached £120,000 a year, was desperate. He had foolishly entrusted his affairs to the three Wildman brothers, who acted respectively as his solicitor, his agent both at home and in Jamaica, and his banker. They had undeniably milked him for years, and the son of one of them had just bought Newstead Abbey from Byron for 90,000 guineas. Fonthill was a nightmare to live in. 'Here it smokes, there the wind blows in – and so would the rain if it were raining', was how Beckford put it. But his fitful financial shrewdness had not deserted him entirely. In 1822 he put the whole estate on the market, and then as now there were those with more money than sense who wanted to be in the news. Christies printed a catalogue which sold 72,000 copies at a guinea each. Only a select few had ever seen Beckford's accumulated treasures, and the sale attracted vast crowds. But two days before it was to take place a notice was put up at the gates stating that the estate, house and all the contents (except for a few of the more remarkable books and treasures) had been sold by private treaty. The buyer, John Farquhar, had made a fortune out of gunpowder, and was able to afford the agreed price of £330,000. But within a year he got another auctioneer, Phillips, to issue another catalogue of the contents, to which Phillips added some inferior items of his own, implying that they had a genuine Beckford provenance. Beckford had discovered that the contractor had never laid the foundations of the tower as instructed, and that it might fall at any time. Farquhar pooh-poohed the warning which Beckford honourably gave him, and sure enough before the year was out the tower came crashing down, destroying the Great Western Hall and the Octagon, but leaving the Eastern Vestibule, the galleries and the Great Dining Room intact. Farquhar, no mean eccentric himself, said he was delighted, because 'now the house would not be too large for him to live in'.

Beckford moved to Bath, by then a rather dingy social backwater where he would not be snubbed by exalted company. He bought two separate houses at the end of Lansdowne Crescent, and joined them together with a bridge which is still there. He then bought an expanse of what was still open country extending a mile to the north of the Crescent, and built a smaller and far more solid tower, containing a few rooms into which he crammed some of his greatest works of art, while the library in the house below was filled with books of great quality and rarity, some of which he had been able to buy back at the Fonthill sale for less than what he had paid for them originally. The tower is crowned with a huge lantern that commands views of an area that stretches from the Mendip Hills to the Cotswolds, and from the Welsh Mountains to the Marlborough Downs. It has been recently renovated with great skill by the Bath Preservation Trust, and the Landmark Trust has created a pleasant flat on the ground floor for holiday lets. Both in Lansdowne Crescent and in the Tower, something of Beckford's individual aura survives.

Beckford's fundamental trouble, from which he never cured himself, was that he had always had so much money that he could, and did, use it to please himself, without reference to others. His literary skill was considerable, but although nothing could have been more romantic than *Vathek*, he could take an intense dislike to other people's leanings in that direction. His comment in the margin of his copy of Percy and Mary Shelley's *History of A Six Weeks Tour Through A Part of France, Switzerland, Germany and Holland* (1817) was as follows: 'Your prose most pompously picturesque Sir is high flown enough God knows but your poetry! Is overwhelming, an avalanche of nonsense – I took it first for blank verse as blank as an unsuccessful number in the Lottery – till certain uncouth jinglings informed me there were attempts at rhyme.'

He lived on to the then exceptional age of eighty-five. Prickly, malign and embittered though he often was in his later years, there is evidence of a much more amiable side to Beckford. He was welcoming and polite to social inferiors from whom he had nothing to fear. But there was bitterness in his inner soul, and scars from the injuries, real or imagined, that he had suffered, whether justly or otherwise. James Lees-Milne's excellent biography which forms the basis for much of the above description is now sadly out of print in its original form: he ends it by reflecting that it is all very well to defy society provided that (like John Christie) you are impervious to society's reactions or, in Beckford's case, revenges. And he ends by drawing a startling parallel between Beckford and his exact contemporary William Blake.

The two men, one extremely rich, the other a near pauper, had diametrically opposed backgrounds and temperaments. But they shared one thing in common, and that was a new intellectual integrity and originality. Each rejected the old, stilted, artificial way of disguising intellectual truth. Blake's methods of building Jerusalem in England's green and pleasant land were visionary and spiritual. Beckford's yearnings were largely pagan and physical. Yet each propounded them in ways that were heartfelt and honest. It is time to consider the eccentricity of Blake.

6

William Blake

(1757–1827)

Both as a poet and a painter William Blake was inspired and original to the point where his sanity was sometimes doubted. Swinburne described him as 'a man perfect in his way, and beautifully unfit for walking in the way of any other man. ... No one, artist or poet, who had any insight or any love of things noble or lovable, ever passed by this man without taking away some pleasant and exalted memory of him', even those who had almost nothing in common with him. Swinburne also considered that all critical opinions of him, except Lamb's, even when well-meaning and inoffensive, were utterly futile, and valueless. Little has changed.

One of the reasons for this was the intellectual context of his life. He was born in 1757, in a street off Golden Square in Soho, and grew up in the so-called Age of Reason; but he was nevertheless possessed by a fervour and fury of religious belief, as is immediately clear from the first glance at his paintings. He survived until 1827, when Wordsworth said, without being patronising, that 'there is no doubt that this poor man was mad, but there is something in his madness that interests me more than the sanity of Lord Byron or Sir Walter Scott.' Samuel Palmer, another visionary artist, reflected that 'if Mr Blake has a crack, it is a crack that lets in the light'.

First and foremost, Blake saw visions. At the age of four, he was terrified by the sight of God looking in at the window; but by the time he was eight, he was coming home from a walk in Peckham Rye and announcing calmly that he had seen a tree full of angels. His father, who was a moderately prosperous hosier by trade, would have beaten him for telling lies, had his mother not intervened. He also saw angels and giants battling in Kentish Town, and watched Robert, his adored brother, who had recently died, ascend to Heaven through the bedroom ceiling. Not surprisingly, Blake came to identify his father with hateful, oppressive authority; but it must be added that apart from discouraging his son's visions, he appears to have been a model father to an unfathomable child.

But to William, the visions were all-important. They seem to have been intensely clear in outline, as were his paintings, in due course. At the age of ten he was sent to Pars's drawing school in the Strand, where he learnt to draw from casts from the antique rather than from life. Hence his strong preference for Michelangelo and Raphael. Indeed, he was assured by the Archangel Gabriel that Michelangelo could draw angels, and Gabriel was in a position to know, since he had sat to Michelangelo. Blake decided to work for an engraver rather than be apprenticed to an eminent painter, which being much more expensive would have given him the feeling that he was taking the bread out of the mouths of his brother and sister. But when his father took him to be apprenticed to an engraver called Ryland, William refused to have anything to do with him. 'I do not like the man's face,' he said. 'It looks as if he will live to be hanged.' Curiously enough, the prediction proved accurate when twelve years later Ryland *was* hanged for forgery. Instead, William was apprenticed to a sound practitioner called Basire, and for a time all went well. But after two years, Blake quarrelled so much with his fellow apprentices that he was sent out to make drawings of the monuments in Westminster Abbey, where he later had another vision, this time of Christ with his Apostles, at the altar. He was often engrossed in his drawing, and came to be teased by the boys of Westminster School, who were at that time allowed to play there. One of them climbed onto the scaffolding where Blake was drawing, and Blake was so enraged that he threw him to the ground. This might have had serious consequences, but by complaining to the Dean Blake actually had the schoolboys turned out of the Abbey for good.

Paradoxically, he held that the supremacy of Homer, Virgil, Milton and Dante lay in the fact that they all addressed themselves to the imagination, which is a spiritual sensation, and only indirectly to the understanding or reason – which is why he detested Newton and anyone else who practised experimental science. For the same reason, he found the Bible 'more entertaining and instructive than any other book'. And one of the most striking things about his visionary eye is how it saw through the limitations of his best known contemporaries, who did indeed attempt to restrict themselves to 'the understanding or reason':

> Mock on, mock on, Voltaire, Rousseau,
> Mock on, mock on, 'tis all in vain!
> You throw the sand against the wind,
> And the wind throws it back again.

Voltaire, with his understandable but empty destructiveness, and Rousseau with his all-absorbing selfishness and self-pity, remain grounded, while Blake soared far above them, however seldom the unworldly world that he created and lived in is accessible to the rest of us.

After his apprenticeship with Basire, he studied briefly at the Royal Academy School, when he objected (among other things) to having to draw from life. In general, he only wanted to paint the artificial constructions of his own mind, but he was content to engrave work by such artists as Flaxman and Stothard. Indeed Flaxman, who was one of the leading sculptors of the day, and who also specialised in illustrating Homer and Dante, among others, was to become one of Blake's closest and most helpful friends. In 1782, having been rejected by his first love, he met Catherine Boucher, and asked her 'Do you pity me?' 'Yes, indeed I do,' was the answer, and he replied, 'Then I love you.' She said later that when she first saw him she knew that he would be her husband, and 'was so near fainting that she had to leave the room'. She was the most patient and devoted of wives, and an excellent housekeeper as well. This was important in view of Blake's complete indifference to money, and his loud protests when it was mentioned. Catherine would give him to eat whatever was in the house, and when there was nothing left would put an empty plate in front of him, so that he knew he must stir himself, rather as in the legend of the Charlton family at Hesleyside in Northumberland, where the lady of the house in former times would serve a spur instead of a joint of beef to the family, and they would take the hint and go out foraging. But as well as her practical good sense she entirely believed what her husband told her, and accepted all his claims and ideas as divine revelation. Blake had to teach her to read and write in the early days of their marriage, and so strong was his spell that in time she, too, saw visions and also learned to draw in a similar fashion to his own.

It was about this time that Blake began to publish poetry which was framed in the conventional style of the day but would take off into his own personal mode.

> With sweet May dews my wings were wet,
> And Phoebus fixed my vocal rage

is typical eighteenth-century stuff, but it is followed by

> He caught me in his silken net
> And shut me in his golden cage.
> He loves to sit and hear me sing
> Then, laughing, sports and plays with me;

> Then stretches out my golden wing
> And mocks my loss of liberty

which could only be Blake.

After the death of his brother Robert, already mentioned, when he saw him arise, 'clapping his hands with joy', William slept for three days and three nights; but thirteen years later he wrote 'I hear his advice and write from his dictate'. This dictation fortunately included instructions for a new method of 'illuminated printing', by a process which was the reverse of etching. The lines to be printed from the copper plate were drawn either in varnish or in some other medium impervious to acid; and the surrounding page area was eaten away to the required depth. This reminds us that Blake was a perfectly capable practitioner when he was not seeing angels in the treetops, and he used this method of printing in all his subsequent books. His more conventional side is also shown in his letters, which have been admirably collected and edited by Sir Geoffrey Keynes. In fact, a better idea of Blake can often be gained by letting him speak for himself rather than by reading what others have said about him.

It was Flaxman who brought Blake to the notice of his two other principal benefactors, William Hayley and John Butts. In 1800, Hayley invited the Blakes to occupy a cottage at Felpham, now a suburb of Bognor Regis but then a charming seaside village where the Blakes were initially blissfully happy. Acknowledging his gratitude to Flaxman for having introduced him to Hayley, Blake wrote as follows:

> It is to you I owe All my present Happiness. It is to you I owe perhaps the Principal Happiness of my life. I have presum'd on your friendship in staying so long away and not calling to know

of your welfare, but hope that now everything is nearly completed for our removal to Felpham, that I shall see you on Sunday.

Then, in visionary vein:

And as the Time is now arriv'd when Men shall again converse in Heaven & walk with Angels, I know you will be pleased with the Intention, and hope you will forgive the Poetry.

To My Dearest Friend, John Flaxman, these lines:

I bless Thee, O Father of Heaven and Earth, that ever I saw Flaxman's face,
Angels stand round my Spirit in Heaven, the Blessed of Heaven are my friends upon Earth,
When Flaxman was taken to Italy, Fuseli was given to me for a season,
And now Flaxman has given me Hayley his friend to be mine, such my lot upon Earth.
Now my lot in the Heavens is this, Milton lov'd me in childhood and shew'd me his face.
Ezra came with Isaiah the Prophet, but Shakespeare in riper years gave me his hand;
Paracelsus and Behmen appear'd to me, terrors appear'd in the Heavens above
And in Hell beneath, & a mighty & awful change threatened the Earth.
The Atlantic War began. All its dark horrors passed before my face
Across the Atlantic to France. Then the French Revolution commenc'd in thick clouds,
And my Angels have told me that seeing such visions I could not subsist on the Earth,
But by my conjunction with Flaxman, who knows to forgive Nervous Fear.

I remain ever yours, William Blake

Mrs Blake wrote another, more accessible, poem to Mrs Flaxman, also thanking her profusely. The following verse gives its more conventional flavour:

> Away to sweet Felpham, for Heaven is there;
> The Ladder of Angels descends through the air;
> On the Turret its spiral does softly descend,
> Thro' the village then winds, at My Cot it does end.

The Ladder is a reference to a water-colour of Jacob's Dream made by Blake about this time, and The Turret was the name of Hayley's own house in the village. Both poems show how visions and more mundane matters could be mixed together in the Blakes' outpourings.

A few weeks later, Blake was writing, in a spirit of contrition for having spoken wildly about religion, to his best patron of all, Thomas Butts, who bought a very large number of his drawings and water-colours:

> I thank you for your very beautiful & encouraging Verses, which I account a Crown of Laurels, & I also thank you for your reprehension of follies by me foster'd. ... in future I am the determined advocate of Religion and Humility, the two bands of Society. Having been so full of the Business of Settling the sticks and feathers of my nest, I have not got forwarder with 'the three Marys' or with any other of your commissions; but I hope, now that I have commenced a new life of industry to do credit to that life by Improved Works.

Sadly, Flaxman could not be persuaded to join in the pleasures of Felpham that summer. He wrote charmingly that 'both Mrs Flaxman and myself should delight in seeing & partaking your cottage delights, but I am bound by my sculpture & cannot make my rocks travel with me'. Far worse was the fact that Felpham turned out to be a damp and unhealthy place in winter, and Catherine Blake became 'so very ill ... the Ague and Rheumatism her constant enemies, & her sickness always my sorrow'. So back they went to London, where by October 1804 she was

> surprisingly recovered. Electricity is the wonderful cause; the swelling in her legs and knees is entirely reduced. She is very near as free from rheumatism as she was five years ago.

And memories of Felpham had become entirely delightful:

> O lovely Felpham, parent of Immortal Friendship, to thee I am eternally indebted for my three years' rest from perturbation and the strength I now enjoy ... O the distress I have undergone, and my poor wife with me: incessant labouring and incessant spoiling what I had done well. Every one of my friends was astonished at my faults, and could not assign a reason; they knew my industry and abstinence from every pleasure for the sake of study, and yet – and yet – there wanted the proofs of industry in my works. ... Dear Sir, excuse my enthusiasm or rather madness, for I am really drunk with intellectual vision whenever I take a pencil or a graver in my hand, even as I used to be in my youth.

A reviewer of the most recent biography of Blake commented that 'he had a supreme lyric gift but an unfortunate tendency to believe in his own pseudo-mythological cosmic system'. To analyse Blake's mysticism and philosophy would be a very long job, and this is not the place for it. But it is worth remembering the strength of his infatuation with the revolutionary spirit of the age that led on from the ideas of Voltaire and Rousseau whom he attacked so eloquently. Another example of his practical effectiveness was the occasion when he almost certainly saved the life of Tom Paine, the author of *The Rights of Man*. Paine had made an inflammatory public speech, at a time of exceptional nervousness and severity on the part of the authorities. He was describing the speech next day to a group of friends including Blake, who told him that if he went home he would be a dead man. In fact Paine's house was already under surveillance and he only just succeeded in escaping to France, the order for his arrest arriving at Dover twenty minutes after his boat had sailed.

Blake showed his theoretical support for the French Revolution by wearing a red cap in the street, but he disliked the attitudes of Godwin, the associate of Paine, almost as much as Newton, and rightly saw in the revolutionary theorists the dreadful seeds of human arrogance and destructiveness which, with the advantage of hind-sight, are so miserably familiar to us today. Nor would he consider compromising with the Philistines, whether spiritual or visual. But he was no friend of organised religion either. He even went so far as to say that 'Prisons are built with stones of Law, brothels with bricks of Religion'. And he firmly believed that 'the strongest poison ever known came from Caesar's laurel crown'.

The chief reason for the loan of the cottage at Felpham was that William Hayley wanted his works illustrated. Blake also decorated Hayley's new library with eighteen heads, including those of Homer, Milton, Ariosto and Spenser. To begin with, Blake was blissfully happy. But the idyll did not last. Apart from those already mentioned, another problem arose when Blake was also involved in a prosecu-tion for sedition. He had rather firmly ejected from his cottage garden a drunken soldier who was supposed to be working in it. In revenge, the soldier accused him of having said 'God damn the King', and that he would support Bonaparte if he came to England. After much anxiety he was fortunately acquitted, according to the *Sussex Advertiser* 'to uproarious applause'.

When he returned to London, neglect and poverty slowly set in.

But Blake didn't care. He thanked God that riches and fame had not come his way, to distract him from his visions and to obscure them. He died three weeks before his seventieth birthday, lying peacefully in bed, and the artist George Richmond, who was there, remembered that Blake was singing songs so divinely that his wife came in to hear better, and he told her 'They're not mine, you know; they're not mine.' Although she had recently said sadly that she 'had very little of his company, he is always in paradise', he now made up for it by telling her that they would never be parted, and that he would go on watching over her just as he had in the long years of their marriage. Then, peacefully, the human spirit left him, as Malcolm Muggeridge, one of his most eloquent admirers, has put it, 'becoming part of the eternity on which his eyes had been so faithfully set during his mortal years'.

To get a true idea of Blake, however elusive, rather than read about him it is far better to ponder on the great collection of his paintings and engravings in the Tate Britain, and to read his poems. Some of his best and most characteristic, in *Songs of Innocence and Songs of Experience*, are often saved from sentimentality by the sudden introduction of strange romantic ideas of his own, as in the most famous of them all, 'Tiger, Tiger, burning bright', and its glorious last verse:

> When the stars threw down their spears
> And watered Heaven with their tears,
> Did He smile his work to see,
> Did He who made the Lamb make thee?

and his contrast between the two kinds of love:

> Love seeketh not itself to please,
> Nor for itself have any care,
> But for another gives its ease,

And builds a Heaven in Hell's despair.

Love seeketh only self to please,
To bind another to its delight,
Joys in another's loss of ease,
And builds a Hell in Heaven's despite.

There remains, also, much that Blake can tell the modern world in his hatred of mechanisation and of the dehumanising effect it has on those who live by it. The victims of these processes can look on him as a wonderful friend. Some progressive acquaintance once showed him a copy of the *Mechanic's Magazine*. 'Ah, Sir,' he said, 'these things we artists hate.' And elsewhere he stated that 'Art is the Tree of Life ... Science is the Tree of Death'. He is the great inspiration of all those who condemn a civilisation that destroys, or goes far to destroying, in man precisely what is most human in him: the expression of his artistic imagination and of his craftsman's skill.

Kathleen Raine once pointed out in a lecture that 'life in harmony with a living nature is Blake's pattern of the good life'. The human figures, the rustic houses and animals in his illustrations to Virgil fit the landscape as perfectly as the sages, fishermen and bridges in the middle distance of Chinese landscape paintings. They belong there more completely than anything else could belong. They are perfect for their context, and their context for them. They are a refreshing and incomparably pleasing reflection for those who are glued to their computer screens, and are enslaved and eventually 'burned out' by them more comprehensively than any toiler in the dark satanic mills of Blake's day.

If his mystical visions often seem hopelessly far-fetched to normal minds, nevertheless it is astonishing that his *Jerusalem* should have been sung with enthusiasm over many decades by tens of thousands of down-to-earth members of the Women's Institute. They might not be confident about driving a chariot of fire; the idea of a bow of burning gold, firing arrows of desire into the air may seem exceedingly remote to them; but it strikes a chord in their hearts and minds that would have faded and been ignored if it were not ultimately genuine. And it is this power to communicate the significance of what cannot entirely be explained that not only makes the eccentric William Blake unique as a visionary poet and painter, but has brought him a kind of immortality.

7

Sir George Sitwell

(1860–1943)

Sir George Sitwell was only two years old when his father died in 1862, but it was not at all long before he became aware of his position in the world. When he was four he was accompanied by his nurse on a train journey, and a kindly fellow passenger asked him who he was. 'I am Sir George Sitwell, Baronet,' was the reply. 'I am four years old and I am the youngest baronet in England.' The other characteristic which this remark indicated was also to remain with him all his life: a total indifference to the impression that he or his words or actions might have on others. In his excellent life of Sir George's son Osbert, Philip Ziegler sums up the former very fairly: 'In some ways remarkably appealing, in some ridiculous, in some curmudgeonly and mean.'

In the case of most of the more distant figures in this gallery, there is often a shortage of interesting detail relevant to their eccentricity. With Sir George there is all too much. For one thing, he wrote a lot himself. And though what he wrote was usually in the form of quite short booklets, they say a lot about his egocentric tastes, and the fact that most of the subject matter is only of interest to a tiny minority does not destroy their value for anyone wishing to understand their author. *Rotherham in the Middle Ages* and *Sheffield in the Wars of the Roses* are among the more specialised; but Sitwell's masterpiece, which is of interest to a much wider readership, and which will be quoted later, was *On the Making of Gardens*. The other great source of information is his son Osbert's vast autobiography, stately and

impressive as some have found it, bloated and stuffed with super-
fluities in the opinion of others. If it dwells more on the absurd and
exasperating side of Sir George's character, it certainly contains many
wonderful examples of his eccentricities. Osbert's feelings towards
his father varied from an early devotion, a middle period of something approaching hatred, and a subsequent mild improvement in
relations; although there were always ups and downs. Certainly,
Osbert's own brand of self-importance created a permanent feeling
that he was hard done by, no matter what his own chronic extravagance might involve.

The value of what was originally a fairly small landed estate was
greatly increased by the discovery of iron and coal – Sheffield is only
seven miles from the family home at Renishaw. The Sitwells had also
married several heiresses but later indulged in wild extravagance in
the late eighteenth century. Careful retrenchment had followed, and
whatever he may have thought, Sir George was never poor. But the
spectre of poverty, and a hatred of extravagance in any field (with the
exception of landscape architecture) hung over him always. As will be
seen, it was made far worse by the extreme wastefulness of his wife,
Lady Ida, and the example of her father, the second Earl of
Londesborough, who got through a fortune of two million, perhaps
eighty million in today's money, without apparent effort. (On coming
into his inheritance he had issued the senior among his innumerable
servants at his various houses with cheque books, so that they 'could
draw on his funds at the bank without worrying him for his
authority'.) The results of this were easily predictable, and it was this
element in his wife's background that was to have perhaps the most
disastrous effect on Sir George's relations with his immediate family.

The problems were made far worse by the fact that he was far
more intelligent than her. Warm-hearted and affectionate, she had
long been hopelessly extravagant in a rather futile way: according to
Osbert, who was fond of her in spite of all her faults, Lady Ida spent

money 'as an expression both of the enjoyment of life and of its opposite: if she felt well and happy, she would order every sort of thing, that neither herself nor anyone else could want. If she felt miserable, then she chose things at random in order to cheer herself.' Anything less likely to lead to a happy married life would be hard to imagine; and after all, a husband was at that time legally responsible for his wife's debts, and her extravagance was such that he could see no way of controlling it.

Ultimately Lady Ida spent on such a scale that she became involved with crooked money-lenders simply because she was too frightened to face her husband. Not that there was anything mouselike about her character. In fact, they had both spent a good deal of the previous few years inventing new ways of annoying each other. But no one would have called her clever. George, on the other hand, though egocentric beyond measure, and often chaotic in his arrangements, was no fool. He was an astute business man, and among his successes was his recognition of the potential of South African shares. Later, two of the cleverest of his sons' friends testified to his intelligence. Alan Pryce-Jones, a gifted communicator who was for many years editor of the *Times Literary Supplement*, recalled that on the rare occasions when he saw Sir George in action, 'he struck me as being a move or two ahead of his children'; while Kenneth Clark believed that '*au fond* they were all jealous of him', not least of his literary style, and expressed their resentment by mocking him on paper, though it must be admitted that he was capable of great financial meanness to them as well. It would also be wrong to omit his consistent unpleasantness to his daughter Edith, even though, with appropriate poetic licence, she may well have exaggerated it, or at least forgotten times when their relations were happier. He never forgave her for not being a son and heir, even when in due course his two sons appeared. But when she was awarded the Silver Medal of the Royal Society of Literature for her poetry, she reported that her father, when informed, 'gave an owl-like hoot of laughter, and said there were far too many poets nowadays'. She added, engagingly, 'I quite agree.'

After his father's death, Sir George spent much of his school holidays at Lambeth Palace, occupied at the time by his great-uncle and guardian Archbishop Tait, who was obliging enough, when Sir George first went to Oxford, to provide him with no less than seventy letters of introduction, all no doubt to dons who were at that time mostly drawn from the clergy. His mother was largely engrossed in religion and works of charity, but had also a very good head for business, and in her long widowhood succeeded in turning round the family fortunes. At the age of twenty-five, Sir George was elected to Parliament, and won two of the seven elections in which he fought. At first, he was the youngest member of the House of Commons, and was consequently invited to the coronation of the Tsar Nicholas II. He was in Parliament for two more years in the 1890s before suffering some kind of nervous breakdown, about the same time as losing a series of lawsuits concerning the coal mines on the Renishaw estate; but probably brought on by the intense activity of his mind and the large number of simultaneous tasks which he was in the habit of setting himself.

Neither Sir George's mother nor the Archbishop had succeeded in restraining his whims in his youth, or teasing him out of his wilder opinions. If his sons ever attempted this, his cross reaction was to reply 'Rude without being funny.' Peter Quennell, a talented writer who became a life-long friend of his children, referred to 'his patrician good looks, the air of dignified remoteness and self-sufficient impassivity with which he travelled through existence'. Apart from that, he had both genealogy and the Middle Ages on the brain, which added to his remoteness and his indifference to the views and sometimes even to the existence of other people. On one occasion, when travelling with his sons in Italy, he wrongly accused his valet of having left the keys to his luggage behind. (They were in fact lying on his dressing-table.) His reaction was to have the locks on all his own and his wife's numerous pieces of luggage forced open in the corridor outside their rooms, as well as those of two large trunks standing outside the doors of adjoining rooms to his own, belonging to two innocent ladies, who were on the point of catching a train. Their belongings had been scattered, and they were in despair. The manager found them other trunks, but Sir George refused to pay the cost involved, and calmly locked himself into his room, remarking to his valet, 'I'm afraid I really can't help other people's troubles.'

This detachment ran beside his conviction that everyone except himself was guilty of the most wanton extravagance, and that financial security depended on cutting himself off from the world. 'Such a mistake to have friends,' he once remarked to Osbert. Yet luckily for him there was one man, his valet Henry Moat, who could, and did, say anything he liked to his employer, and indeed to anyone else. Osbert was to describe him as 'an enormous purple man like a benevolent hippopotamus ... He had eighteen brothers and one sister. They came from a line of whaling captains dating from the time of Elizabeth I.' Later on, when Henry Moat had become acclimatised to life in Tuscany, he also claimed that his family had originally been called Moatti, and had migrated to Yorkshire from Italy. (So at least Osbert was told; but is it possible that some at least of Henry's claims were an elaborate tease on the children, gently reflecting his employer's obsessive concerns with family origins?) Just occasionally Moat would confide unexpectedly in friends of the family: 'Sir George is the strangest old bugger you ever met,' he once observed to the composer Constant Lambert, who was staying at Renishaw.

In 1909, after giving up his seat in Parliament, Sir George purchased Montegufoni, a palace in Tuscany containing over two hundred rooms, from which he conducted his extremely thorough study of Italian gardens and garden architecture, as well as creating a magnificent garden of his own. On one occasion he had planned a large dinner party at the Castle, and by the time the guests were an hour and a half late his patience ran out: he said, 'Henry, if they don't arrive in ten minutes I shall sit down to dinner, if necessary by myself.' Henry replied, 'Well, Sir George, you couldn't ask for more cheerful company, could you?' Another slight complication arose when several of the Italians working at the Castle, including the acting chauffeur, the son of the bailiff, and the plasterer, all happened to be called Guido. One morning, Moat inquired, 'Any orders for the motor today, Sir George?' 'Yes, Henry. Tell Guido to drive into Florence, to help Guido with the painting. Guido can wait while Guido has luncheon, and then Guido will go back to Florence and fetch Guido here.' 'Sir George, if you are going on like that, I had better give notice before my mind gives way.'

Luckily for them all, although Henry did leave for a time, it was to go to an employer who was intolerable in quite a different, unrelieved, way, and he returned to the Sitwells after 1918. Sir George always referred to Henry as 'the Great Man', and Henry's own attitude swung irregularly between exasperation and veneration. When alterations at Montegufoni were being endlessly planned, and then replanned, and then started all over again, Henry wrote to Osbert:

... and now Sir Geo is annoyed but as you know never satisfied and will not leave well alone changes, makes a muddle of things and then blames other people. We are supposed to be going to the Castello the 1st of May, but you should just see it now many floors up laying hot water pipes and new drains it will not be ready to go into properly for another 2000 years if G.R.S. has the managing of the works.

On the other hand, in 1929, travelling with Sir George in Germany, Henry wrote another of his many revealing letters to Osbert:

... very interesting it is Sir George taking me with him to see the Castles, Palaces, Museums and Pubs. (Last two words crossed out.) We have become well known in Germany ... visiting the above places over and over again and giving the attendants the hell of a time so that when they see him they scatter like scalded cats some through doors, some through windows and others up the chimneys one fat old woman wanted to take his umbrella from him and then commenced a vigorous tug of war result the fragments of the umbrella has been sent to the Castle (Montegufoni) to be put away in the armoury ... But joking apart Sir George is very good to me and took me to Potsdam. Very interesting. In the ex-Kaiser's private palace in Berlin we saw the table on which he ordered the mobilisation of his Army and Navy 'I.VIII.XIV at 5 o'clock' the table is made from the oak taken from Nelson's ship the *Victory* and for the writing paper envelopes etc. to stand in there is a model of the *Victory*. There is also a beautiful atlas globe of the World in the Kaiser's study and I showed Sir Geo where you was in Spain.

(At the Hohenzollern Museum) of course I marched behind him and really I think and others say so too that if possible Sir George looks more distinguished than ever and the attendants eyed him intensely the head one especially and we had all of them bowing and scraping. The head guide ordered a special catalogue to be brought and given to Sir George and then he came and asked me his (Sir Geo's) name I felt very proud of him.

Now dear Master Osbert take great care of yourself ...

Master Osbert was by then aged nearly thirty-seven, but his friendship with Henry Moat was to remain one of his greatest pleasures, partly perhaps because in the North of England in general, relations between masters, however grand and otherwise haughty, and servants were inclined to be more free and easy than elsewhere. A few years later, Sir George's grandson came to Montegufoni at the age of four or five accompanied by a much loved Jamaican nanny. Henry Moat regarded her as inquisitive and bossy, and one day when she inquired what was for lunch, 'Let me see,' came the answer, then, after a long pause, 'Slices of cold boiled Missionary it is today.' After that, according to Osbert, Nurse Cole (for that was her name) became 'notably more subdued in manner'.

On the day before he died, in February 1940, Henry Moat wrote a last letter to Osbert. It began:

> It did me good to see your fist again, and really you write a good hand now. (Osbert's handwriting had always been deplorable.) ... I had a nice letter from Sir George reading between the lines he has every hope of living a good many years yet if he is going to see the perfection of his new gardening scheme he often told me he would like to see 80 now I think he is heading for 100. I was rather tickled about him going into the Blue Nuns Home for fear of hurting their feelings I don't think it is habitual of him considering others feelings.

Interesting though it is to see Sir George through the eyes of others, as well as through his own idiosyncratic observations, to return to the family's life before 1914, an example must be given of the happier relationship that occasionally existed between Sir George and his elder son. In the summer of 1908 he had decided to send the fifteen-year-old Osbert off with a tutor to Rome, but at the last minute could not resist accompanying them himself. To quote Ziegler, 'in three gruelling days they visited the Forum (twice), the Capitol, the Palatine (twice), the Pantheon (twice), St Peter's (three times), the Borgia apartments, the Pope's garden, the Church of St Cecilia, the best Greek statues in the Capitoline and National Museums, the Appian Way, the Colosseum (twice), the model of ancient Rome restored, the cascades at Tivoli, the Villa d'Este, and a good many other things.' Osbert passed this marathon test with flying colours. 'It is charming to find how strong Osbert seems to be,' wrote Sir George. 'No amount of travelling or sightseeing tires him ... He is such a dear boy altogether.' Osbert enjoyed it all hugely, and remained a tireless sightseer all his active life – unlike so many who have been force-fed in this way in youth; but he never gave his father the slightest credit for having introduced him on such a grand scale to pleasures of this kind.

In 1914 there came a family catastrophe that was to have a shattering effect on all of them. Lady Ida had become involved, through a military acquaintance of Osbert's, with a money-lender or broker of loans called Julian Field. Not only had Field been made bankrupt a few years earlier, but he had also received a prison sentence for forgery. Nearly all of the loans obtained by Field for Lady Ida remained in his own pockets, as a result of her complete ignorance of business or money matters of any kind, and although her debts only amounted to about £2,000, she actually signed documents making herself responsible for £30,000. Field reckoned that her husband would pay up whatever was demanded of him, rather than allow his wife to face a lawsuit in public. But he reckoned without Sir George, who had come to hear of a previous similar case in which a twenty-year-old cousin of the Sitwells had been similarly entangled by Field, and his parents had paid the price of silence. Apart from his alarm at the idea of being responsible for her debts, Sir George took the view that had these parents refused to pay, and had the case come into court, Field would have been shown up and punished, and Lady Ida would not have fallen into his clutches. Therefore, in his merciless view, it was his duty to let his wife be prosecuted in order to render Field harmless for the future. She initially won several of the cases brought against her. But in the end, even though her actions and letters had been nothing more than grotesquely careless and unbusinesslike, a guilty interpretation could be put on them, and she went to prison for fraud for three months early in 1915.

Osbert, in the Grenadiers, was in the trenches in France, in constant danger of his life. The second son, Sacheverell, was an already unhappy schoolboy at Eton, and the whole family was plunged into acute misery at Lady Ida's unjust fate. Naturally, they blamed their father; but it is very doubtful if he could have foreseen the result of his chilly, ruthless devotion to principle.

In the successful policy of retrenchment in the previous century, the family had abandoned Renishaw and spent most of the time, when they were not in London, at a smaller but still substantial house in Scarborough. On the day before Osbert was to leave for the front, his parents were subjected to the heavy naval bombardment of Scarborough by the German fleet. Sir George, with most of the household, had taken shelter in the cellar, and cautiously emerged when it was over. In the middle of a nearby public park there was a large pond, containing an island on which stood a rustic hut. If the German fleet were to return, and land, Sir George's carefully considered plan was to take refuge in the hut for as long as the Germans remained in Scarborough. Years later, he reflected that, 'I should have been quite happy, too, with a few books down from the London Library' and then followed an often repeated, veiled reproach: 'I never *allow* myself to feel bored!'

His genius for self-absorption was also displayed in a letter of advice which he wrote shortly afterwards to Osbert at the front:

> ... though you will not, of course, have to encounter anywhere abroad the same weight of gunfire that your mother and I had to face here ... yet my experience may be useful to you. Directly you hear the first shell, retire, as I did, to the Undercroft, and remain there quietly until all firing has ceased. Even then, as one grows older, a bombardment is a strain on the nervous system,

Colonel Charles de Laet Waldo Sibthorpe, 1842

Charles Waterton at age 42

John Christie, 1954

William Beckford

William Blake

Sir George Reresby Sitwell, c 1900

Edward Lear

Lewis Carroll

Lady Hester Lucy Stanhope

Victoria Woodhull

'Sir Iain Moncreiffe of that Ilk.'

but the best remedy for that, as always, is to keep warm and have plenty of plain, nourishing food at frequent but regular intervals. And, of course, plenty of rest. I find a nap in the afternoon most helpful, if not unduly prolonged, and I advise you to try it whenever possible.

Ever your loving father, George R. Sitwell

Though he can have had little opportunity to test his father's advice, Osbert mercifully survived the war, but he never forgave Sir George for the humiliation that his mother had suffered. As a consequence Osbert's affection and respect for his father had died. Osbert now owned Renishaw, but did not have the money to keep it up. Consequently he was always in debt. As Sir George saw it, in Philip Ziegler's well chosen words, Osbert insisted on keeping up an expensive house in London even though he only lived in it for a few months each year, and from his ivory tower made not the slightest attempt to relate his increasingly lavish tastes to his income. And in 1930, Sir George, whose favoured plan was still that Osbert should replace him in Italian exile, produced a variant on this plan. His new game, Osbert told Hollingworth, the agent at Renishaw, was 'Musical Chairs'. All the employees at Renishaw, whether they liked the idea or not, were to be sent to live at Weston, the Sitwell house in Northamptonshire which had been Sachie's home since 1927. The servants and gardeners at Weston, for their part, were to move to Renishaw. Sachie was to go to Renishaw, Osbert to Montegufoni, while Sir George himself would take over the Tudor dower house at Long Itchington, near Rugby, which had been freed by the death of his sister Florence. Hollingworth replied that he was amused to hear of the project: 'After all, it was not more fantastic than some of the ideas one has heard in the past from the same source.' Such a remark, coming from an eminently sane and loyal employee, shows how impossible

Sir George could be; Osbert behaved ungenerously, even ungrate-fully, but he was not unprovoked.

Lady Ida, after thirty years of being on almost perpetually bad terms with her husband, died in 1937, and Sir George was 'too tired' to attend her funeral. But his fatigue soon wore off, and in the hope of distracting him from his favourite pastime of giving unwanted advice in copious quantities to his sons, they found a companion-secretary for him called Francis Bamford, a serious young man who shared his employer's endless interest in genealogy. Later in the same year, Sir George decided that he, too, was dying, and summoned Osbert to Montegufoni. Osbert reported, truthfully or not, that he had 'seldom seen him looking so well, and in such high spirits'.

However, towards the end of 1940, after Italy had declared war on the Allies, but with Sir George being left in peace at Montegufoni, he fell seriously ill, and had blood transfusions. He was now befriended by a retired Swiss banker called Bernard Woog, with whose bank he had deposited funds in Zürich. When he came out of hospital he moved into the Blue Nuns' Nursing Home, giving rise to Henry Moat's final quip, already quoted. Making himself as difficult as ever, he decided that the nuns were over-charging him, and quarrelled with the Mother Superior. The Italian authorities now questioned whether he was really ill at all, or whether he could be interned with other British residents. Nor did he show any signs of dying, which had earlier seemed a possibility.

The Italians said they would have no objection to his moving to Switzerland, but naturally dug his toes in: 'I dislike running away from difficulties even if threatened with starvation if I stay,' as he put it in his usual self-centred way. After raising various other objections he eventually agreed to what was required of him, and settled in Locarno. But he was not done for yet. 'I have never known anything like his zest for life,' wrote Osbert, 'I keep on getting telegrams demanding books and saying how happy he is.' He next indulged in a flirtation with his German nurse, who had a reputation for extracting money from vulnerable patients. She was promised an annuity of £500 a year, and to Osbert's alarm rather fancied the idea of becoming Lady Sitwell. Woog, however, for the time being proved his worth as far as the family were concerned by persuading the Swiss authorities not to renew the nurse's residence permit, and the danger was averted. By the end of 1942, Woog reported that Sir George was now getting rather keen on her replacement. Then, in June 1943, he peacefully died. It was suspected that Woog had to some degree feathered his nest, and after Sir George's death a number of financial questions were left unanswered.

Enough has already been said of Sir George's contrariness, his often chaotic way of life, his distortion of facts, and above all his unremitting selfishness. It is worth dwelling briefly on his achievements. What he designed and carried out in the formal garden at Renishaw and Montegufoni was truly remarkable: the hedges, statues, vistas and lake are admired to this day by thousands of visitors. What he designed in his mind and did not get round to carrying out was more remarkable and extravagant still. If his ideas were not entirely original, his adaptations of Italian traditions of design were carefully and successfully thought out, and the results are his finest memorial. And although he expressed them in the Pateresque idiom of an already bygone age, he showed a remarkably, and perhaps surprisingly, sensitive touch in recording his thoughts on his favourite subject. ('Flying shafts of silvery splendour fall upon the fountain, save for the strange light that is burning in the chamber window.') The last page of *On the Making of Gardens*, especially its closing description of the statue of Neptune, makes a fitting end to this sketch:

Nature, like a shy wood-nymph, shall steal softly back on summer nights to the silent domain, shading with tenderest pencillings of brown and grey the trellised arbour, painting with cloudy crusts of crumbly gold the long balustrades, inlaying the cornices with lines of emerald moss, planting little ferns within the fountain basin and tiny patches of green velvet upon the Sea God's shoulder. ...

8

Lady Hester Stanhope

(1776–1839)

In 1803, when Blake was returning to London from the seaside joys of Felpham, a totally different form of eccentric was moving into 10 Downing Street, to act as hostess for her uncle, William Pitt the Younger. He was forty-four, Hester Stanhope was twenty-seven; neither of them was married. The founder of the Pitt dynasty, 'Diamond' Pitt, had made a great fortune in India a century earlier, and according to Hester's great-nephew, the Prime Minister Rosebery, the family blood 'came all aflame from the East and flowed like burning lava to his remotest descendants with the exception of Chatham's children, but even then it blazed up again in Hester Stanhope.'

When she was only four, her mother, Pitt's sister, had died. Her father, Earl Stanhope, had soon remarried, and his attention was entirely taken up with radical politics and scientific inventions. He spent twenty years perfecting a prototype steamship which the Admiralty accepted, needless to say, with the greatest possible reluctance. In politics, though the brother-in-law of Pitt, he had been violently against the American War of Independence, and in favour of the French Revolution, becoming Chairman of the Revolutionary Society in London in 1788. He had discarded his titles, and the badges of his rank, and had removed the coronets from the entrance gates at his home at Chevening, though later, when he modified his opinions, they were replaced. (The house is now the grace and favour residence of the Foreign Secretary.) He had protested publicly to the

93

French about their treatment of their negro slaves, and in the House of Lords had moved the recognition of the French Republic. His motion was of course rejected, and he had withdrawn from Parliament until 1800, when he proposed peace with Napoleon.

As an inventor, besides his steamboats, he devised a method of stereotyping, and other printing machinery, which were acquired by the Clarendon Press at Oxford in 1805. In 1777 he invented two calculating machines, and later a microscope lens for testing the skins of fever patients. Perhaps his most dramatic discovery was a method of fire-proofing for buildings. To illustrate its merits (and his own outstanding eccentricity), he had a wooden house built, and invited a party of friends to assemble on its upper floor. Surrounding the house with combustible materials, he set fire to it and, according to the *Philosophical Transactions of 1778* 'the flames rose around to a height of 87 feet, yet the friends (who must have had their misgivings) did not suffer the slightest inconvenience'. Hester inherited her father's acute intelligence and curiosity, as well as other more imperious characteristics. Not knowing what fear meant, she was quite unafraid of her father, though in the later words of his granddaughter, 'ardently though he advocated liberty and enfranchisement abroad, he was the sternest of autocrats at home'. But, as she later claimed, 'I could always govern my father better than any body, because I could bear his oddities with more patience, and could *joke* him into things which plain sense and argument would have failed in.'

Hester was a difficult child, made more difficult by the treatment she received. She spoke of the 'eternal warfare' which she waged against all French and German governesses. A family friend recalled that 'her early education had much to do with her eccentricities. Her father, believing in manual labour, had set her regularly to tend turkeys on a common.' And in order to improve their posture, Hester and her sisters had their backs 'pinched in with boards that were drawn tight with all the force the maid could use.' Otherwise their father and stepmother took very little interest in them and left them to the mercy of the servants – and took no interest in the servants either. Hester recalled that 'My father once followed to our own door in London a woman who happened to drop her glove, which he picked up. It was our governess; but, as he had never seen her in the house, so he did not know her in the street.' 'He always checked any finery in dress. If any of us happened to look better than usual in a particular hat or frock, he was sure to have it put away the next day, and to have something coarse substituted in its place.'

She once managed, by a subterfuge, to attend a great military review at their neighbour Lord Romney's. 'The King took great notice of me ... and when he came towards us "Where is she?" he would cry. "I hear them laughing, and where they are laughing, I must go too." When he was going away, he wanted to put me bodkin between himself and the Queen. "My dear," he said to her, "Lady Hester is going to ride bodkin with us. I am going to take her away from Democracy Hall." ' The Queen was not amused, and the idea was dropped.

Perhaps exasperated by their resistance to his tyranny, Lord Stanhope was later to disinherit all his children. He had already behaved monstrously to Lord Mahon, his eldest son by his second marriage, and had refused him any sort of decent education, in the strange hope that he could keep him so firmly under his thumb that when he reached the age of twenty-one he would allow his father to dispose of the Chevening estate as he pleased. But the father reckoned without his formidable daughter, who when she had grown up moved in with her grandmother, Lady Chatham, the widow of the elder Pitt, who lived mostly at Burton Pynsent, a backwater deep in Somerset. Hester felt a strong sympathy for Lord Mahon, and combining that with her passion for mystery and intrigue, she determined, if at all possible, to rescue him. With the financial help of

Francis Burdett (who had married the daughter of the banker Coutts) and a charming young diplomat called Francis Jackson, who produced passports and letters of credit as well as exalted introductions, she made it possible for him to escape from Chevening. This he did, in the winter of 1801, with the help of a loyal servant; and though messengers were sent after him in hot pursuit, he reached the Channel before them, and by the end of March was safely enrolled as a student at the University of Erlangen. Hester was warmly congratulated by the rest of the family, the Grenville cousins and others, who were heartily sick of her father's tantrums and tyrannies.

Her uncle, William Pitt the Younger, had once been asked what would happen to Hester when her grandmother died. He had replied sternly, 'Under no circumstances could I offer her a home in my own house.' Yet when the time came he took her in without a murmur, and she sat at the head of his table. Her brother commented that 'he came to regard her with almost a father's affection, and she formed for him a strong and devoted attachment, which she extended to his memory as long as her own life endured.' Her niece, the mother of the Prime Minister Rosebery, thought that 'her wit was certainly even then far too satirical, and too little under control'. Nor were actions any less boisterous than words. In later life, General Sir William Napier recalled a visit to Pitt at Putney, where he had a house.

Mr Pitt liked practical fun, and used to riot in it with Lady Hester, Charles and James Stanhope and myself; and one instance is worth noticing. We were resolved to blacken his face with burnt cork, which he most strenuously resisted, but at the beginning of the fray a servant announced that Lords Liverpool and Castlereagh (who Hester once dismissed as 'his monotonous lordship') desired to see him on business. 'Let them wait in the other room', was the answer; and the great Minister instantly turned to the battle, catching up a cushion and belabouring us with it in glorious fun. ... after ten minutes' fight we got him down and were actually daubing his face, when with a look of pretended confidence in his prowess he said, 'Stop, this will do; I could easily beat you all, but we must not keep these grandees waiting any longer.' ... We were obliged to get a towel and basin of water to wash him clean ... the basin was hid behind the sofa, and the two lords were ushered in. Instantly, Mr Pitt's tall, ungainly, bony figure seemed to grow to the ceiling ... for some time they spoke; he made now and then some short observation ... and finally dismissed them. Then, turning to us with a laugh, caught up his cushions and resumed our fight.

Pitt died in January 1806, and Hester lost her best friend in the world, as well as what had briefly been her home. He left instructions for a pension of £1,200 a year to be left to her, honourably dictating a note that he was 'far from saying that my public services have earned it, but still I hope that my wishes may be complied with'. Her two sisters also received £600 each. On the grounds of his public opposition to Pitt, Hester foolishly refused to accept a further royal grant proposed by Fox, which would have added several thousand pounds to her small income. But apart from her personal loss, her situation was completely changed. Her niece observed that 'she had been accustomed to queen it in society, to be courted, consulted and applauded, and she could not endure to find herself now of little or no account ... and resented it as an unmerited humiliation. ... she became irritable, suspicious of slights, and ready both to give and take offence, discarding some of her friends and alienating others' including her uncle Lord Chatham, Lord Grenville and Mr Canning. Downing Street had made her more inconsiderate and arrogant than ever, and her fall was all the harder.

Much worse was to follow. Shortly before Pitt's death, her heart had been broken by Lord Granville Leveson-Gower, who had left in relief for the embassy in St Petersburg rather than face her impetuous attentions. But she now became strongly attracted by Sir John Moore, the commanding officer and benefactor of her brother Charles in the Peninsular War, and an 'understanding', if not an engagement, arose between them – or so at least it seemed to her. Moore executed a masterly retreat to Corunna when threatened by a great advance by the French after Salamanca. He embarked his sick and wounded at Corunna, and even without his guns defeated Soult's army on 18 January 1809, but was himself mortally wounded. On his deathbed, he murmured to his ADC, Hester's youngest brother James, 'Stanhope, remember me to your sister.' The shock to Hester, when she received the news, was appalling, and was redoubled when she learnt, a few days later, that her brother Charles had also been killed at the very same time as her beloved Moore. Her health broke down, London became unbearable to her, and she retired for the summer to lodge at a farm in Glen Irfon, a remote Welsh valley which she had visited the previous summer on a picturesque expedition from Bath. She learnt to look after, and milk, a cow (called Prettyface). She became very popular locally, and made many permanent improvements to the farmhouse, though after she left, the bath which she had installed was used as a corn-bin.

What was she to do? London disgusted her, and what made it even worse was that in her grief she attributed the deaths of her two loved ones entirely to what she saw as the infamous and treacherous mistakes made by Pitt's successors. Rather than linger there, without friends or influence, she decided to accompany her surviving brother James back to his regiment in Spain. A change of scene, no doubt, seemed better than nothing; but when she sailed from England, she can have had no inkling that it would be for ever.

After narrowly escaping shipwreck off Trafalgar, they landed at Gibraltar and James went off to join his regiment at Cadiz. At this point a young man called Michael Bruce, fourteen years Hester's junior, who was travelling with Lord Sligo, attached himself to her party, at first on a casual basis; but their connection was to ripen into a full-blown affair in the course of their stay in Malta, where there was a lot of English society, and where she was made very welcome by the Governor, General Oakes. Bruce was the son of a rich Scottish banker in London. In the shady gardens of the Palace of Sant' Antonio they fell in love, and at the age of thirty-four, for the first and almost certainly the last time, Lady Hester took a lover. Quickly realising that Bruce's father was not likely to be best pleased with this state of affairs, she wrote him a brave and quite extraordinary letter.

Sir,
If your character inspired me with less respect, I should not give you the opportunity of perhaps accusing me of impertinence, in presuming to address you upon a subject that requires all my courage to touch upon, and great liberality on your part ... You may have heard that I have become acquainted with your Son, his elevated and Statesman like mind, his brilliant talents to say nothing of his beautiful person, cannot be contemplated by any feeling mind with indifference, to know him is to love and admire him, *and I do both*! Should you hear this in any irregular way, you might not only mistake the nature of the sentiments I feel towards him, but my *views* altogether, & imagine that he had fallen into the hands of an artful woman who wd. take him in, as far as it lay in her power. Sir, you need not be under any of these apprehensions, the affection I feel for him wd. only prompt me the more to consider his advantage from every point of view, & at this very moment (while loving him to distraction) I look forward to the period when I must resign him to some thrice happy woman really worthy of him. ... I shall then, like a dethroned Empress, resign to virtue the possession of that perfection which she alone has a right to ... Sir, if you knew me,

I flatter myself that it wd. be unnecessary to give you any further assurance of the sincerity of my intentions, but as you do not, there is *no promise however solemn* I am not willing to make on this subject. It wd. be a satisfaction to me to learn (tho' I do not wish you to write to me) that this candid confession of my sentiments has not displeased you. Do not however Sir *mistake* the tone of humility that I have adopted thro' this letter, which proceeds in fact from my being one of the proudest women in the world, so proud as to despise the opinion of the world altogether, *as far as relates to myself*, but when I am addressing the parent of a man who I so tenderly love (and for whom he has so great an affection) a sacred sort of reverence steals upon my mind, which I hope has communicated itself to my expressions, as I have intended they should convey the confidence and respect with which I have the honour to remain

    Yours etc. etc.

    Hester Lucy Stanhope

It is a remarkable letter for any woman to have written, let alone one whose formal education had consisted of minding turkeys on a village green, and it says a lot (among other things) for the infectious eloquence of the company she had kept in her Downing Street days. Michael Bruce also wrote to his father, a dutiful letter, but of a less remarkable kind. He was a serious young man, on excellent and affectionate terms with his father, and so far from lounging about the Mediterranean, he was engaged on a quite impressive course of study both of ancient and modern history and of current affairs, as a means of fitting himself for a public career of some kind. The letters were written in June 1810, and it was not until December that answers to them were received (both dated 20 August). Craufurd Bruce's reaction was a mixture of pride that the granddaughter of the great Chatham had fallen for his son, and a feeling that she, better than anyone else, could develop his intellectual qualities and his chances of success in the world. To her he wrote 'my son wrote me that as he had found you much cleverer and better informed than his other Companions, he had left them and ascribed himself to your Party, you have therefore intentionally or not made yourself responsible for his future character and achievements in life ... Our correspondence has certainly commenced on a very extraordinary footing.'

It was to go on in the same fashion, at too great a length to be quotable. It is enough to say that, quite predictably, the problem was going to be money. Hester had very little, and was wildly extravagant; Michael only had what his father gave him, and before the idyll ended, it was going to cost more, in chartered boats, rented houses, servants and a high standard of living, than his unfortunate father can ever have expected. Michael and Hester never appear to have quarrelled, but by October 1813, when their life together was leading nowhere, she effectively packed him off home, escorted by her faithful Greek servant Georgio. She was for a time deeply sorry to lose him, and sent many a loving message in his wake, rather like a fond mother sending her son back to school. There was also practical advice: 'Remember also never to cover your saddle with an oil cloth, unless it is lined, as the wax will stick and make your ride very uncomfortable when it is taken off, a skin is a much better thing.'

But this was all far in the future. After the Maltese idyll became established, the heat became too much for Hester, and she and Michael embarked on a frigate, the *Bella Paola*, for Patras, and from there to Corinth, where they fell in again with Lord Sligo, who was travelling in some style. They all crossed the isthmus together, Sligo's retinue including a Tartar, two superbly arrayed Albanians, equipped with silver-stocked pistols and silver-hilted yataghans; a dragoman; an artist to record views and costumes, a Turkish cook, and two English servants in livery. All, except Hester and her maid, were armed to the teeth. After a spell in Athens, where she saw a good deal of Byron, but was impressed neither by his person nor his poetry, they embarked, unwisely as it turned out, on a Greek cargo boat which ran into a serious storm in the Sea of Marmara. But they reached Constantinople safely, and Hester rented a house for the winter at Therapi, on the Bosporus. She was very well received by Stratford Canning, the British Minister, who later recorded that 'her conversation had strong attractions for me, not withstanding its measureless exuberance and the not infrequent singularities it displayed'. She told Canning that Sir John Moore had had grave reservations about his command in Spain, and that General Phipps had called on Pitt one day and disparaged Moore. Enraged by his comments, she had said, 'You imagine, General, that Mr Pitt does not greatly value Sir John's abilities, but learn from me, you nasty kangaroo (alluding unkindly to Phipps' paralytic infirmity, and his manner of holding his hands) that there is no one in the King's army whose services he appreciates more highly!' 'Lady Hester, Lady Hester! What are you saying?' exclaimed Mr Pitt, with an ill-suppressed smile 'which betrayed his secret enjoyment of the scene'.

Hester's love of giving was as strong as her intolerance, and she told Canning that if Lord Plymouth, who was ill in Constantinople, required the services of the doctor who she had brought with her, he was welcome to them. 'I never saw his Lordship,' she said, 'and I detest his mother, and only act towards him as I should do to the most perfect stranger. Therefore pray do not make any fine speeches for I should very much dislike to do anything which might in future bring on an acquaintance. But any medicines that he cannot get here he is welcome to. ... I return you your papers and letter with many thanks ... but I never believe anything I read in the *Gibraltar Gazette*, for I know for certain that articles for that paper have been fabricated in the Foreign Office and sent out there to be printed, and afterwards recopied into English newspapers, as "extracts of letters from Gibraltar from the *Gibraltar Gazette*." '

Sadly, after ten months of sunny relations, she fell out with Canning as heavily as she was to do with almost everyone else who was, for a time, a friend. It arose from a report that she had been seen walking on the sands in the company of the French *chargé d'affaires*, in order to obtain through him a passport for France, since she was 'dying to see Napoleon with her own eyes'. Canning remonstrated with her, and she made things worse by telling him that she hadn't wanted to embarrass him in view of his youth. (He was ten years younger than her.) She even wrote to Lord Wellesley saying that 'Mr Canning is young and inexperienced, full of zeal but full of prejudice ... the above reason induced me to see M. de Latour-Maubourg privately.' She even sent a copy of this patronising letter to Canning, who broke off relations with her for himself and all his staff. Her reaction was to declare that she believed that Canning was jealous of her because she had 'made my own way with the Turks, and that the Pasha's brother, brother-in-law and Captain of the Fleet, had dined with us ... I must likewise tell you that Canning has been much shocked at my having gone on board the fleet in men's clothes,' adding sardonically that 'a pair of overalls, a military great coat, and cocked hat, is so much less decent a dress than that of a real fine lady in her shift and gown, and half-naked besides!'

Happily, the quarrel was soon made up and Canning bore no malice, assisting her when she was later shipwrecked on Rhodes. The passport for France having been refused, she and her party decided to press on to Egypt, but the Greek vessel that they chartered sprang a leak in a violent storm and their long boat was nearly wrecked as well. They were stranded on a rock in torrents of rain for thirty hours without food or water before landing on the shore, where their boat was dashed on the rocks and foundered just after they had landed. They were then still three days' journey from the town of Rhodes, 'over dreadful rocks and mountains'. Because of adverse winds, they reached Rhodes exactly a month after leaving Constantinople on 23 October, and were then driven back there by yet another storm. Having lost all her belongings in the wreck, Hester was obliged to buy simple Turkish costumes, which she described in a letter to her lawyer in London: 'a sort of silk and cotton shirt; next a striped silk and cotton waistcoat; over that another with sleeves, and over that a cloth short jacket without sleeves, beautifully worked in coloured twist, a large pair of breeches, and Turkish boots, a sash into which goes a brace of pistols, a knife and a sort of short sword, a belt for powder and shot made of variegated leather, which goes over the shoulder, the pouches the same, and a turban of several colours, put on in a particular way with a large bunch of natural flowers on one side. This is the dress of the common Asiatic; the great men are covered with gold and embroidery, and nothing can be more splendid and becoming than their dress.'

The Bey being 'the only disagreeable Turk I ever met – once a slave and now a tyrant, ignorant, sordid and vulgar', she managed to rent a house three miles outside the town: 'Let those who envied me in my greatness now envy me in rags; let them envy that contented and contemplative mind which rises superior to all misfortunes which are independent of the affections of the heart.' Her luck now turned, and Captain Henry Hope of the frigate *Salsette* came to the rescue of the party, and after the usual delays from storms they finally reached Alexandria in February. 'This place I think quite hideous,' she wrote to General Oakes, so after a little very necessary shopping, off they set, first by donkey, then in flat-bottomed boats, for Cairo. There a magnificent reception awaited them from the Pacha, who had been informed of Hester's illustrious background. She dressed the part, in a Tunisian costume of purple velvet embroidered with gold, and a Kashmir turban and girdle.

She had another narrow escape from drowning when returning

across the Nile from a visit to the Pyramids. Water was pouring through the planks of the ferry; the boatman panicked, but recovered his wits and rowed them ashore after being threatened by an English servant, who had torn off his turban and plugged the leak.

In May 1812 Hester sailed on, for once without mishap, to Jaffa, from where she began a long trek on horseback via Jerusalem, Bethlehem and Acre. At Nazareth her horse fell, injuring one of her legs so badly that she had to spend a week in the Franciscan convent. At Sayda she somehow received an invitation from the Prince of the Mountain to visit him at Dayr-el-Kamar, in the Lebanon. He sent an escort of twelve camels, twenty-five mules and four horses, as well as an armed escort for her protection. Her method of making herself welcome was unusual but effective.

I purchased from a Druse an immense sheep, the tail weighing eleven pounds, and desired it to be taken to a village, where I ordered the people to assemble and eat. When I arrived the sheep was alive. The moment it was killed, it was skinned and brought in raw upon a sort of dish made of matting, and in less than half an hour it was all devoured.

I understand feeling my ground so well with savage people, that I can ask questions no other person dares to put to them; but it would not be proper to repeat here those I asked even the *sages*, and still less their answers. Anyone who asks a religious question may be murdered without the Prince of the Mountain or the Governor being able to punish the offender.

... the Governor has proved a Lucifer, and I am the first traveller he ever allowed to walk over his palace, which has been the scene of several massacres ... he judged it necessary to make one of his chief officers taste out of my cup before I drank, for fear of poison; but I am used to that; yet this man on his knees before me looked more solemn than usual.

Moving to Damascus, she was warned that she must wear a veil at the risk of being insulted. But as her niece put it, 'any suggestion as to what she should, or should not, do, invariably aroused Lady Hester's opposition. She declared that she would enter Damascus in broad daylight, dressed as she was – and she did.'

> My entry was reckoned so dangerous, because of the fanaticism of the Turks (about the dress and behaviour of women) ... (Having first lodged in the Christian quarter) we found ourselves in the most distinguished part of the Turkish quarter. I went out in a variety of dresses every day, to the great astonishment of the Turks; but no harm happened. ... A visit to the Pacha on the night of Ramadan was magnificent indeed. Two thousand attendants lined the staircase, etc. ... The message of invitation was accompanied by two fine Arab horses, one of which I mounted. But I am sorry to say they are both dead of the glanders.

All this was at a time when no native Christian could venture to leave his quarter or even show himself in a conspicuous garment or turban without running a good chance of having his bones broken by some zealous fanatic or other.

Hester now decided to visit the legendary ruins at Palmyra, partly because she was told on every side that it was impossible. As she put it in a letter to General Oakes,

> Everybody is surprised at my courage, as above eighty thousand Arabs will be on the march in a fortnight, and I have determined to go straight into one of the largest Bedouin camps. ... A report has been in circulation that fifty thousand Wahabees are within four days' journey of this city; but I do not believe it. It takes rise from a letter from Mecca to the Pacha, saying *several* thousand dromedaries mounted by Wahabees have set off, not improbably

for this place, which they once before attempted to take, but were driven back, after having burnt and ransacked every village on the road. But the strongest tribe of Bedouin Arabs – my friends – who do not like the present Pacha, will probably join any party against him, and there will be a fine confusion in the desert, as well as here. But luckily for me, I am well known to some thousands, who have seen me with their chief visiting their horses ... But yet, when disturbances take place, few are safe. If the worst should come to the worst, I shall take fifty of them and set off to my friend Emir Beshyr, the Prince of the Mountain, where I shall be quite safe. He has one hundred thousand troops at his disposal, which he can assemble in three days, and nothing was ever so kind as he has been to me. (It is a good thing that Mr North is safe off, or he would be in a sad fright.) I am not at all, knowing my own presence of mind under all circumstances, and I have excellent friends in this country. Be perfectly easy about me; my good luck will not forsake me when any confusion takes place.

To Canning, in Constantinople, she wrote in the same super-confident vein, but added more prudently, but perhaps not more accurately:

... they have all been disputing who should escort me, and since the great battle in which 100,000 horses took the field it is very dangerous to make yourself *over* to either party, because you might run the risk of being cut to pieces by the hostile tribe; but I go with a chief who plays into the hands of both, and I shall be friends with all, until I see which I like best, then I shall declare myself for that tribe. I am quite delighted with these people, and I seem to take their fancy.

She had various other distractions at Damascus that are worth mentioning:

The other day I was paying a visit to the wife of a very great Effendi (who, though not the most agreeable, is the cleverest man I know here), not less than fifty women were assembled in the harem to see me, when in came the lord and master – all put on their veils except his wife and his own women, he made a sign, and all retired. We talked some time and then he proposed dining ... in a beautiful court paved with coloured marbles, with fountains playing among the orange trees. Everything was served in high style by black female slaves, and a black gentleman. Immense gilt candlesticks, with candles nearly six feet high, and great illumination of small elegant lamps suspended in clusters in different parts of the court. The proud man fetched a great book to talk astronomy, upon which he asked me ten thousand questions, keeping me there till nearly ten o'clock, an hour past the time when, if any one is found in the streets, they are to have their heads cut off – such is the new Pacha's decree. ... The Pacha cuts off a head or two nearly every day; but yet I do not think he has added much to his own security, for he is by no means liked, nor does he command half so much as my friend the old Delebache.

When Hester finally left Damascus for Palmyra on 20 March, her retinue consisted of the following: the two sons of the King of the Desert, forty camels loaded with provisions and water and presents, twenty horsemen, the doctor, Mr Bruce, two dragomans, a Mameluke, two cooks, a Caffagi, four Cairo sayses, the Emir El-Akoar, a stud-groom, Mr Bruce's valet, Madame Fry, two sakas or water-carriers, her slave, two tent-pitchers and an escort of Arabs. There was some anxiety arising from the wild rumours that had circulated about her wealth, and consequently about the possible ransom that might be had if she were to be captured by enemies. She was said to ride a horse worth forty purses, with saddlery and stirrups of pure gold; to receive every morning one thousand sequins from the English Sultan's treasurer; to carry a book indicating where hidden treasure was to be found (it was in fact Wood & Dawkin's *Views of Palmyra*); and to possess a herb which transmuted stones into gold.

After visiting various tribes on the way, they reached Palmyra, which at that time had about fifteen hundred inhabitants. The chief and about three hundred people rode out two hours' distance to meet them, armed with matchlocks and guns, all surrounding her and firing them off, with savage shouts and much music and dancing. When they arrived, the space before the triumphant entrance arch was filled with dancing girls, 'most fancifully and elegantly dressed, and beautiful children placed on the projecting parts of the pillars with garlands of flowers'. When they moved on, 'the lancemen took the lead, followed by poets from the banks of the Euphrates, singing complimentary odes and playing upon various Arabian instruments.' To crown it all, 'the loveliest of the living statues' bent down from her pedestal to place a wreath on Lady Hester's head.

At Bethlehem a prophetess had told her, 'You will be crowned Queen of the East.' And so, in a sense, she was. But in the words of her biographer Joan Haslip, who, though friendly to her subject, is not swept away by her:

> her empire was but the sands of the desert instead of the teeming streets of the sacred town ... It was the crowning point of her restless, aimless life ... she was to appeal to generations of romantics. But it was she who gave the orders to the Sheik that no European should be allowed to visit the ruins without the payment of a thousand piastres, ... so that only a few of her compatriots could share in her glory. Even in the wilds of the desert Hester Stanhope worshipped before the altar of her colossal egoism. She had Zenobia's fame, her beauty and

personal charm, her masculine bravery. But where were the legions for her to command? Where were Longinus and the laden elephants bearing her the spoils of Egypt and Palestine? She had nothing on which to expend her restless, feverish energy. ... There was very little of the explorer or the archaeologist in her make-up. All she searched for was power, and the unquestioning admiration of a tribe of ignorant Arabs was more gratifying to her than the friendship of her equals. From now on she styled herself 'Queen of the Desert', and as long as she paid handsomely for that privilege, no one bothered to contradict her.

The chief trouble was money. Earlier, Michael Bruce's father had produced a total of over £1,000 to keep the young lovers going, but naturally this dried up when his son came home. Hester seemed to think that she had some kind of divine right to expect endless funds from Mr Coutts, her grandfather's old friend, but there was a limit to his good will.

The only trouble was that the King of the Desert was at war with a powerful tribe, who thought they could ransom Hester for 25,000 piastres. But, except for one minor skirmish, they were not seriously attacked. Far more dramatic, however, was an episode on the way to Palmyra that Hester does not mention in her letters to General Oakes or her cousin Henry Williams Wynn. She and her party were suddenly abandoned in the evening by the whole of their escort, and they were left, by her niece's account, 'in the heart of the desert, without guide or bearings, knowing neither where they were, nor how to find the wells on which their existence depended, encumbered with a great pile of luggage, most tempting as booty, and so few in number as to be at the mercy of any strong band of marauders.' The situation was extremely critical; but Lady Hester, undismayed, appeared 'as cool as if in a ballroom'. She gave orders that every man should take his gun and pistol, and stationed her little garrison at different points round the camp. After a while, however, Nasar (the Emir, and leader of the expedition, who had moodily taken against her and moved away with his troops) reappeared, and it was shrewdly suspected that he had been no further off than some neighbouring sandhills, behind which he had watched the effect of his proceedings. The whole scare was, in fact, a feint to test Lady Hester's nerve, and see whether she could not be frightened into paying a larger subsidy. When this little game came to nothing, the whole expedition apparently moved on as before. She afterwards claimed that although Bruce's aim had been to inspect the ruined splendours of Palmyra, hers had, all along, been to 'see the Bedaweens to perfection'.

I like the fine arts, yet to say the truth, I am much more interested in the works of God than those of man. These savages, guided by their own wonderful abilities, and who have reduced the wants of human nature to a mere nothing, gave us a most wonderful example of mental and bodily strength. Besides, the beauty of parts of the desert in early spring are not to be described. Almost all the bulbous plants we rear with so much care spring up in a fortnight as if by magic, bloom amongst innumerable, unknown, odoriferous herbs, and fade, nearly as quickly, by the great heat and drying winds.

This passage in her large correspondence explains how she chose to see herself and her motives. But, no doubt, like many other wilful characters, she pretended to rationalise what was far from being entirely rational, and often made up her mind that she had all along intended to bring about what had come to pass largely by chance. She had rejected, and been rejected by, a society and a system for which her imperious, generous spirit, with its curious blend of indepen-

111

dence, pride, integrity, scorn and intermittent common sense was entirely unfitted. From then on, she was always going to go her own way, occasionally satisfying her appetite for power and prestige, as fate would let her.

Sadly, however, the fickle Arabs were only interested in providing her with escorts and triumphs as long as she paid. She settled for a time in a convent called Mar Elias near the cost at Latakia. For some time after Bruce left for Vienna, Paris and London, she sent loving and impressive letters after him, which he answered in an increasingly unsatisfactory fashion. Many of her letters to him, from all periods, are printed in *The Nun of Lebanon*, edited in 1951 by Ian Bruce. They throw a much fuller light on the violent contradictions in Hester's nature than can be fitted in here.

She succumbed to the plague in November 1813, which had reached the port of Latakia and cut it off from mails and other shipping, and that, combined with the departure of Bruce, had a further unsettling effect on what was already a hopelessly unpredictable and irrational nature. It must be mentioned that for most of her long life in the East she had the company of an exceptionally loyal and long-suffering doctor, C.L. Meryon, who gave up a great deal of his life to looking after her, and was often bitterly abused for his pains, above all when she was suffering, (as was he in a milder form) from the plague, which laid her low, and nearly killed her, in November 1813, not long after Bruce's departure. By June she had to some extent recovered, though not without taking a violent dislike to her unfortunate maid, Anne Fry, who could do nothing right. When the poor woman remonstrated mildly, she was outraged, and told the doctor that 'he had no more spirit than a louse, else he would have knocked that damned woman flat a thousand times rather than stand by while she was being insulted'. In the opinion of Joan Haslip 'her normal life was now finished, and from now on her existence was one of fantastic delusions and imaginary triumphs' – not that these had been altogether missing before. She soon also casually mentioned in passing in a letter to Bruce that 'Prince Kasan the Emir's eldest son has sent me a live *tiger*, which I have tied up in my yard, well secured. I rather think it will go off with the Ship, as the sailors say they know how to make it quite tame ...'

By the beginning of the following year, 1815, Hester undertook a project which even by her standards was exceptionally grandiose and ill considered. Someone had given her a copy of an old document giving the location of a very large amount of hidden treasure under an old temple at Askalon, on the coast not far from Gaza. This was not as far-fetched a story as it sounds: property was often insecure in an area where a rapacious pacha was capable of seizing the worldly goods of some poor wretch who had offended him. But Hester's idea was indeed wild, namely to find the treasure and hand it over to the Sultan, at the same time light-heartedly deciding (without the least confirmation) that the search would be financed by the British Government. In her grand way, all she asked for was the personal glory of conducting a successful expedition, and national kudos for England by performing a magnificent service for the Sultan.

However her excavations at Askalon yielded up nothing more than a fine late Roman marble statue of a warrior. In a fit of frustrated disappointment she had it destroyed, and all she could then do was to scatter coins to the workmen and distribute lavish presents among her suite of governors and consuls. She also dismissed the troop of astrologers and magicians that her increasing interest in the occult had inspired her to take into her services.

At this stage Hester began to receive occasional European visitors, naval officers and French diplomats among others, and an English traveller named William Silk Buckingham, who arrived 'in a state of extreme illness and exhaustion'. Hester insisted that he remain for nine days to recover his strength, and he succeeded in gaining her fullest sympathy and attention. When he got home he recorded, perhaps somewhat naively, in his book of travels that: 'If to be sincerely and generally beloved by those among whom we reside, to possess power and influence with those who govern, and to have abundant opportunities of exercising these for the weak and helpless, be sources of delight, it may safely be concluded that Lady Hester Stanhope is one of the happiest of human beings.' It was not everybody's experience of her, but it shows what charm she was still capable of, when she chose.

Other notables attempted to visit her, few of them successfully. One failure was the Princess of Wales; Hester disliked other women on principle, and successfully avoided her by making a sudden trip to Antioch.

Another visitor was the French romantic poet Lamartine, then in his thirties, who later became an ineffectual head of the French Government after the revolution of 1848. His approach was flowery, and successful:

> Milady, like you I became a traveller and a stranger in the East;
> like you, I have only come in search of the beauty of nature, of
> ruins, and of the works of God ... I shall reckon as the most
> memorable day of my journey the one on which I shall have met
> the woman who is herself one of the marvels of the East.

His description of the evening that he spent with her must be taken with several pinches of salt, but may well contain elements of truth: the fierce Albanians hanging round the courtyards; the squalling cats, regarded by her Ladyship as sacred animals; (why do so many remarkable women have such an unworthy weakness for these conceited, unresponsive animals?) In Hester's cloister, according to Lamartine:

> It was so extremely dark that only with difficulty could I distinguish her noble, grave, yet mild and majestic features. The lady
> appears to be about fifty years of age but possesses those pecu-

liar features which age cannot alter: freshness, colour and grace depart with youth; but when beauty resides in the form itself, in purity of expression, in dignity, in majesty, in a thoughtful countenance, whether in man or woman, beauty may change with the different periods of life, but it does not pass away; such is the person of Lady Hester Stanhope.

It is a graceful tribute. Hester was always grateful for an audience for her accounts of her heavenly visions but, though she enjoyed his company, Lamartine was mistaken if he thought he had made a great effect. Yet he conferred considerable fame on her for a new generation when he later published his *Souvenirs de l'Orient*:

Lady Hester is not mad: madness, which is written so strongly in the eyes, is not expressed in her beautiful and amiable look. ... [but she may make use of] a voluntary madness, conscious of itself and acting from peculiar motives. The strong admiration which her genius has kindled, and still attracts among the Arab population, is but a policy. ... They require a commerce with the stars, with prophecies, miracles and the second sight of genius ... perhaps like all beings endowed with powerful intellectual faculties, she deceives herself as well as others ...

Lamartine may have had an absurd side, but he was not stupid, and this analysis of her descent into a regular reliance on mumbo-jumbo is distinctly convincing. But his opinion was not shared by an Arab sage who declared that she certainly was mad, because she put sugar in her coffee. It was a world of subjective standards.

But of all those who made their way to Djoun, the one to give the most enthusiastic and useful account of Hester was Alexander Kinglake, the author of *Eothen*, whose mother had been a neighbour of the Pitts long before at Burton Pynsent. On the strength of this connection she agreed to receive him, but was unwilling to talk about Somerset when she had another rare audience for her rambling tales of sorcery and magic and the stars. Kinglake bore all this manfully, and was rewarded from time to time when she tired of the role of prophetess and became, in his words,

> the sort of woman that you sometimes see in London drawing-rooms – cool, decisive in manner, unsparing of enemies, full of audacious fun, and saying the downright things that the sheepish society around her is afraid to utter. ... In truth this half-ruined convent, guarded by the proud face of an English gentlewoman, was the only spot throughout all Syria and Palestine in which the will of Mehemet Ali and his fierce lieutenant were not the law. ... And so long as Chatham's granddaughter breathed a breath of life, there was always one hillock, and that too in the midst of a most populous district, which stood out and kept its freedom.

Nor had Hester lost her famous powers as a mimic: after twenty-five years she delighted Kinglake by recalling every one of the despised Byron's mannerisms. Kinglake did not visit her till 1835. But back in 1820 a kind of civil war had broken out on the fringe of the Pashalik of Acre, and Lady Hester was not going to stand by and ignore the refugees who came to her door, and whose homes were devastated and whose vineyards had been destroyed. The little convent at Mars Elias was too small for the purpose of cherishing them, so she moved to the ruined monastery of Djoun, above a narrow mountain valley in the heart of Lebanon. Doctor Meryon, who knew her better than most, felt that 'she chose to dwell apart and out of the reach of that influence and restraint which neighbourhood and society necessarily impose upon us'. In other words, she wanted the absolute power which is only available in isolation. She pawned many treasured possessions, furs and snuff-boxes, to pay for her building activities and to help the destitute, whether high or low. Needless to say, her plans were not on a modest scale. In Joan Haslip's words, there were:

> walls within walls, with long, twisting corridors connecting a long series of detached cottages; secret courts and gardens with winding staircases; stables and covered paddocks, hidden spyholes, and trap-doors through which refugees might escape. What had been a small ruined monastery now assumed the aspect of a warlike fortress. Once the gates were opened, one entered into an enchanted paradise, scented gardens with marble statues overgrown with morning glory, splashing fountains beneath pergolas of jasmine and roses, clematis and periwinkles reflecting in clear pools of water.

Eagles and vultures swooped overhead, and jackals howled outside her gates. What better setting for Hester Stanhope's type of eccentricity? But not all of her dreams and fantastic prophesies were mistaken. A somewhat deranged French general called Loustenau, who shared her addiction to the occult, foretold with her the earthquake at Aleppo in 1822. His son, an idle adventurer and sponger, for a time obtained some hold over Hester, as he reminded her, in some faint and confused way, of her adored General Moore. But Loustenau junior died before much harm could ensue. Medicines based on astrology were an increasing threat to Hester's general stability, and what she called asthma but which was in fact consumption forced her to give up riding, so that she could no longer make an impression on the peasants by galloping over the mountains in her dazzling robes. But her devotion to her two Arab mares, which no one was allowed to ride, became an obsession. She borrowed money at exorbitant rates of interest from merchants in Sidon and Beirut, and ruin was slowly approaching.

But still her spirit held out. She was outraged when the Emir had her camels confiscated in order to transport marble from Sidon to Iptedin, but the convoy made the mistake of pausing at Djoun, and in the space of half an hour she gave orders for all the marble slabs to be smashed to pieces. Men were killed at her gates in order to intimidate her, and further verbal threats from the Emir were intended to induce her to leave the country. Hester laughed them to scorn with a fearless dismissal of the messengers: 'Let them tell their masters that she cared not a fig for his poisons and daggers, and that if he sent her his son to make terms with her she would gladly kill him with her own hands.'

Eventually, and inevitably, her creditors, or one of them, caught up with her. A certain Mr Homsy had found that all his letters to Hester, and to the British Consul at Beirut, were ignored. He eventually applied direct to Mehemet Ali, who in turn applied to Colonel Campbell, the British Consul-General in Alexandria, who corresponded with the Foreign Office for no less than three years, and who was described, for his pains, in the last letter which she wrote in her life, as a 'blackguard toady'. As long as Wellington was in power, no drastic action followed. But when Palmerston became Foreign Secretary, he had no patience with her, and orders were given preventing the annual signature of her life certificate, without which her pension, granted by her uncle's wish, could not be paid. In 1837 she had reached the age of sixty-one, and what would once have been a passion of fury turned to withering contempt. She wrote the following letter to the newly crowned eighteen-year-old Queen Victoria. Of all her wild utterances, this surely is the most surprising:

Madam. Your Majesty must allow me to say that few things are more disgraceful and inimical to royalty than giving commands without examining all their different bearings, and to cast aspersion upon the integrity of any branch of a family who has faithfully served their country and the House of Hanover.

As no inquiries have been made of what circumstances induced me to incur the debts alluded to by Your Majesty's Secretary of State for Foreign Affairs, I deem it unnecessary to enter into any details or explanations upon the subject. But I shall not allow the pension, given me by your Royal Grandfather, to be stopped by force. I shall resign it for the payment of my debts, and with it the name of an English subject and the slavery at present annexed to it.

She sent Dr Meryon to England, to publish her recent correspondence. Alas! her day was done. When published in the press, her complaints aroused little except ridicule and hostility. Only her old friend Sir William Napier, a veteran of Moore's last campaign, and the historian of the Peninsular War, came to her defence in a letter to *The Times*. He stated that 'in early life he was an inmate of Mr Pitt's house when Lady Hester was the mistress of it and when those who now insulted her would have been too happy to lick the dust from her shoes'.

It was to be Hester's last satisfaction. Her health went from bad to worse, water poured in through the roof of her apartment, she was surrounded by worthless, tormenting servants. There was no doctor near. She died, more or less alone, on 23 June 1839, and was buried on her lonely mountain.

By the end, haughty pride and stubborn independence, which had deprived her of all ordinary comforts and conveniences, were all that was left to her. When these failings had not been operating at full strength, and before her illusions of representing her country in a fashion in keeping with her forebears had set in, she could be sensible, well-informed and shrewd. Sadly, her splendid courage had worn out and the wherewithal for her generosity was exhausted. It is difficult to imagine a more poignant end.

9

Lewis Carroll and Edward Lear
(1832–1898 & 1812–1888)

Most of the characters sketched here so far have been eccentric in
their actions or their attitudes to other people. With Lewis Carroll
and Edward Lear, two of the best loved fantasists of the nineteenth
century, it was more a question of their deeply original use of words.
It is worth examining what they shared and how they differed in their
powers of imagination and expression.

Carroll spent his professional life as a mathematician at Christ
Church, Oxford. His boyhood had been spent in a very happy family
circle in the rectory at Croft, on the borders of Yorkshire and
Durham. His father, the Revd Charles Dodgson, as well as being a
highly conscientious pastor, who had at one stage opened a village
school out of his own meagre funds, also possessed a vivid sense of
fantastic fun, of which the following letter to his eight-year-old son
is a striking example.

My dearest Charles,
I am very sorry I had not time to answer your nice little note
before. You cannot think how pleased I was to receive something in your handwriting, and you may depend on it I will not
forget your commission. As soon as I get to Leeds I shall scream
out in the middle of the street, *Ironmongers, Ironmongers*. Six
hundred men will rush out of their shops in a moment – fly, fly
in all directions – ring the bell, call the constables, set the town

121

on fire. I will have a file, a screwdriver and a ring, and if they are not brought directly forth in forty seconds, I will leave nothing but one small cat alive in the whole town of Leeds, and I shall only leave that because I am afraid I shall not have time to kill it. Then what a bawling and tearing of hair there will be! Pigs and babies, camels and butterflies, rolling in the gutter together – old women rushing up the chimneys and cows after them – ducks hiding themselves in coffee-cups, and fat geese trying to squeeze themselves into pencil-cases. At last the Lord Mayor of Leeds will be found in a soup plate, covered up with custard and stuck full of almonds to make him look like a sponge cake that he may escape the dreadful destruction of the town. Oh! Where is his wife? She is safe in her own pin-cushion with a bit of sticking plaster on the top to hide the hump in her back, and all her dear children, seventy-eight poor little helpless infants crammed into her mouth, and hiding themselves behind her double teeth. Then comes a man hid in a teapot, crying and roaring, 'Oh, I have dropped my donkey. I put it up my nostril, and it has fallen out of the spout of the teapot into an old woman's thimble and she will squeeze it to death when she puts her thimble on.'

At last they will bring the things which I ordered, and then I spare the town, and send off in fifty waggons, and under the protection of a thousand soldiers, a file and a screwdriver and a ring as a present for Charles Lutwidge Dodgson from
his affectionate Papa

It is hardly surprising that the boy turned out as fanciful as he did. Like his father, Charles was a hard worker, who shone in his undergraduate work, the only real cloud appearing when his mother, who had given him every kind of love, and of sympathy in his less than happy school days at Rugby, and general all-round encouragement, died soon after he went up to Oxford. With her something very important went out of his life. But he took his first-class degree in Mathematics in 1855, and not long afterwards became a Student of Christ Church (or what would anywhere else be called a Fellow). He soon began to apply himself to the new and satisfyingly exact science of photography: 'It is my one recreation,' he wrote in his diary, 'and I think it should be done well.' But it was to be more than a recreation. The historian of the subject, Helmut Gernsheim, was later to say that Dodgson was 'the most outstanding photographer of children in the nineteenth century, and after Julia Margaret Cameron the most distinguished amateur portraitist of the mid-Victorian era.' And it was in going into the Dean's garden to take a photograph of Christ Church Cathedral that he first set eyes on Alice Liddell, one of the daughters, then aged four, of the new Dean, whose appointment a few years before he had described as 'not having given much satisfaction in the college'. It was this sight that was to lead Charles to his huge success both as a photographer and as the creator of *Alice in Wonderland*.

Since the days of his very happy family circle at Croft, he had always got on well with other children, first his own brothers and sisters, and soon with others that crossed his path. He continued to do so; and when the Dean and his wife went to Madeira for Christmas he went to 'nursery dinner' at the Deanery and began to photograph the children. But the episode which was to lead to *Alice in Wonderland* took place when he took three of the Dean's daughters, then aged thirteen, ten and eight, for an outing on the river; the fifth member of the party being Robinson Duckworth, a Fellow of Trinity and later Dean of Westminster. Years later, Charles would recall the 'cloudless blue above, the watery mirror below, ... the three eager faces, hungry for news of fairyland ... from whose lips "Tell us a story, please!" had all the stern immutability of fate.' Alice enjoyed the story so much that when they all got back to Christ Church she

123

exclaimed, as they said goodbye, 'Oh, Mr Dodgson, I wish you would write out Alice's adventures for me.'

In a strange reversal of roles, it was Alice who fathered *Alice*, Charles who formed the story in his fruitful and exact brain, and brought it into the world. When she grew up, Alice married, produced a family and lived happily ever after. *Alice*, the book, spread and multiplied in an infinitely fecund fashion, enough to satisfy the most demanding mathematician. As well as several translations into all the European and Scandinavian languages, there are versions in Chinese, Esperanto, Braille, Russian, Hebrew and Gaelic, and two in shorthand. There are four Japanese translations and six in Chinese, though it has to be said that General Ho Chien, Governor-General of the province of Hunan, issued an edict in 1911, forbidding the use of the story in schools, on the grounds that speaking animals were 'degrading to man'. There have been musical settings, including Erik Satie's unforgettable *Le Chapelier S'Etonne*. Although Charles was a great opera and theatre-goer, after his first ballet at Covent Garden he declared that he never wished to see another. Yet a ballet based on *Alice* was performed at the Festival Hall in 1953, and was hugely enjoyed. One of the very few failures of *Alice* was the Walt Disney film version, which hopelessly failed to reproduce the subtle spirit of the original, and was nothing more than a noisy travesty. Of the book itself, in English, about 180,000 copies were sold in Charles's own lifetime, and by 1911, with the appearance of cheap editions, the sales figure had risen to 659,000.

Obviously, Charles's contradictory appetite for the company of little girls, which was, anyway for a time, reflected in their insatiable demand for his stories, has been looked on with suspicion. But it must be said that there is no shred of evidence that Charles's affection for them had any element of physical paedophilia. Had there been, it is inconceivable that the Liddell parents, and others, would have allowed their children to visit him, usually alone, or be taken by him on boating expeditions and picnics. The children, at least at first, greatly enjoyed his avuncular kindness as well as his almost magical talent for telling stories and elaborate jokes. And his invitations must have provided exciting breaks in what was often a strictly controlled and monotonous upbringing, especially for children who were not natural bookworms. Of course, the Victorians were often guilty of excessive control over children who must be seen but not heard, and must accept bedtime without protest, but it is hard to see them falling for the absurd overreaction of today, when hysterical rules prevent children from sitting next to grown-ups on long air journeys. For all the strictness of their mothers, and the often callous behaviour of nannies and governesses, many middle- and upper-class children of the nineteenth century led freer lives than those of today. And, of course, they were never exposed to the often stultifying onslaught of the modern media on their whole existence.

There remained, however, a theory in the Hargreaves family, into which Alice married, that Charles had wanted to marry her. It was an age of long engagements, and it was not uncommon for young men to ask permission from a girl's parents to 'aspire to her hand', beginning even as early as the age of fourteen or so. It is clear that Mrs Liddell was a considerable snob, and whatever Charles's cerebral gifts might be, he was not good enough for Alice, and not likely to become so. She therefore put a stop to the idyllic picnics and since Charles believed implicitly that looks and gestures of love should never be exchanged between a man and a woman before parental approval had been first obtained, that was that.

However, his career as a photographer carried him into exalted circles. First, the Tennysons in the Isle of Wight, who he had met through photographing the poet's wife's nieces at Croft Rectory, and later the poet himself and his two sons while on holiday in the Lake District. Sadly, Charles managed to annoy Tennyson by asking his permission to keep some verses that Tennyson had not wanted circulated, and although he visited Farringford, Tennyson's home in the Isle of Wight, his attempts to move onto closer terms with him were unsuccessful, and he had to be content with taking pictures of the house and its surroundings.

Charles was ambitious. No doubt his dismissal by Mrs Liddell was a spur to his desire to mix with celebrities and, of course, to take their photographs. His sitters included Ruskin and Ellen Terry, as well as Gabriel and Christina and William Rossetti; and he scored a near miss with the Prince of Wales, who was in residence at Christ Church in 1859. But he succeeded somehow in getting some of his photographs shown to Queen Victoria, and heard from a lady-in-waiting that 'the Queen admired them very much, and that they were such as the Prince would have appreciated very highly and taken much pleasure in'. In 1869, to amuse three sisters called Drury, he composed a fake letter purporting to come from the Queen, inviting him to a Garden Party at Buckingham Palace. He later also took photographs of Prince Frederick of Denmark, the brother of the Princess of Wales, and thought him 'a much brighter specimen of royalty than his brother-in-law'. Like innumerable artists before and since, he did a number of nude studies, including several of a favourite model, Frederick Leighton, and before his death, for whatever reason, he left instructions to his executors that nine of these were to be destroyed. He made his feelings perfectly clear in a letter to the artist Harry Furniss in connection with his illustrations for *Sylvie and Bruno*. 'I *wish* I dared dispense with *all* costume; naked children are so pure and lovely.' Virtually all his nude drawings were of girls of about five years of age, and when in 1888 he drew a naked girl of fourteen, who had had nine years experience of modelling, he recorded in his diary 'I think a spectator would have to be really *in search* of evil to have any other feelings about her than simply a sense of beauty, as in looking at a statue. ... It was a real enjoyment to have so beautiful an object to copy.' His biographer Derek Hudson, who shows consistent good sense and understanding of his subject, has commented that he seems to have owed much of his remarkable success in photographing little girls to his habit of, in a sense, falling in love with them. Precisely in *what* sense remains unknown. Perhaps he did not even know himself, or perhaps it varied from child to child. But what is not in doubt is that the later memories of the children that knew him, some of whom were still alive when Hudson wrote his life, were singularly consistent and uniformly happy.

It is clear that there was also a sense in which the earnest young mathematician, who took Deacon's Orders in the Church, never grew up to reach emotional maturity. But what did happen was that after 1860, when he published a forbidding volume entitled *A Syllabus of Plane Algebraic Geometry*, he embarked on what Hudson calls 'a great flood of print' which was to flow for the rest of his life. Mathematics, logic, university odds and ends, games, puzzles, children's stories and light verse: he simply couldn't stop. From this time on, Charles also compiled a Register of Correspondence, listing details of every single letter that he wrote or received until January 1898, a total of 98,721 documents, with a further five thousand items relating to his work as Curator of the Senior Common Room. His eccentricity was therefore mixed with formidable amounts of energy and most enviable powers of meticulous organisation. But to provide a more vivid portrait against the above background, it is worth quoting some of his more characteristic and engaging flights of eccentric fancy.

Soon after the publication of *Alice*, a small child called Agnes Argles, daughter of the Dean of Peterborough, was egged on by family and friends to write to 'Mr Lewis Carroll', as Dodgson had by then become. (Lewis Carroll being a sort of inversion and adaptation of his two real Christian names, Charles Lutwidge.) Writing to inquire when he was going to write another book, she received the following answer.

I have a message from a friend of mine, Mr Lewis Carroll, who is a queer sort of creature, rather too fond of talking nonsense. He told me you had once asked him to write another book like one you had read – I forget the name – I think it was about 'malice'. 'Tell her,' he said, 'that I have just written a little story which is printed in *Aunt Judy's Magazine* and that I have ordered a copy to be sent to her.'

'Very well,' I said. 'Is that all the message?'
'One thing more,' he said, as a few tears trickled down his cheeks, 'tell her I *hope* she isn't angry with me for talking nonsense about her name. You know I sometimes talk nonsense ...' ('always', said I) – and if she *was*, I hope she has forgiven me by this time!' Here the tears came showering over me like rain (I forgot to say that he was leaning out of an upper window, talking to me) and, as I was nearly wet through, I said 'Leave off that, or I won't send her any message at all!' So he drew in his head and shut the window.

If you have any message for him, you had better send it to
Yours very truly,
Charles L. Dodgson

But like anyone else, he did not like being ignored; especially by little girls. On 13 March 1869, he wrote to Mary MacDonald, the daughter of a close friend, as follows:

Well! You *are* a cool young lady indeed! After keeping me waiting all these weeks for an answer, you quietly wrote on another subject ... I wrote ... on the 26th January last, offering you a copy of the German edition of *Alice*. Well, the days rolled on, and the nights too (as nearly as I can remember, one between every two days, or thereabouts) and *no answer* came. And the weeks rolled on, and the months too, and I got older, and thinner, and sadder, and still NO ANSWER came. And then my friends said – how white my hair was getting, and that I was all skin and bone, and other pleasant remarks – and – but I won't go on, it is too dreadful to relate, except for all these years and years of waiting and anxiety ... still NO ANSWER ever came from this granite-hearted young person! And then she calmly writes and says, 'Oh, do come and see the race!' [The Oxford and Cambridge Boat Race, visible from the MacDonalds' house.] And I answer with a groan, 'I *do* see the race – the human race – it is a race *full of ingratitude* – and of all that race none is more ungratefuller, more worser – more – my pen chokes, and I can say no more!

It is worth, at this point, tantalising those who know German, by quoting the opening verse of the brilliant and faithful translation of *Jabberwocky*, one of the finest nonsense poems ever written. It was the work of Dr Robert Scott, the collaborator with Dean Liddell in the Greek Lexicon that has never been superseded.

> Es brillig war. Die schlichten Toven
>   Wirrten und wimmelten im Waben;
> Und aller-mumsige Burggoven
>   Die mohmen Rath' ausgraben ...

But to return to the letter quoted above, it may contain an explanation of why Charles's friendships sometimes ended rather abruptly, though not bitterly. Children do not like grown-ups to make heavy weather about small matters. And though his tone remains playful and teasing, it may have all seemed a little too much; a little too contrived, a little too facetious, a shade too insistent. And indeed, a little Lewis Carroll at a time is the best way to consume him, except in the beautifully structured and brilliantly inventive case of *Alice* itself. There the story is too perfect in its way for one to select one particular extract rather than another, in a book of this kind. But in the case of *The Hunting of the Snark*, published in 1876, twelve years after *Alice*, and five after *Through the Looking Glass*, it is perhaps worth quoting its ending, where the threat of disappearance that hangs over the Hunter in the event of the Snark turning out to be something else, more sinister, fatal even, comes true, and the poor Baker is gone. Whereas the earlier passages are good rollicking stuff, perhaps rather inspired by the *Bab Ballads* of W.S. Gilbert, there is something mysteriously and genuinely poetic about the conclusion, hinting at an underlying wistfulness beneath all the fun and jokes.

'It's a Snark!' was the sound that first came to their ears,
    And seemed almost too good to be true.
Then followed a torrent of laughter and cheers:
    Then the ominous words 'It's a Boo –'

Then, silence. Some fancied they heard in the air
    A weary and wandering sigh
That sounded like ' – jum!' but the others declare
    It was only a breeze that went by.

They hunted till darkness came on, but they found
    Not a button, or feather, or mark,
By which they could tell that they stood on the ground
    Where the Baker had met with the Snark.

In the midst of the word he was trying to say,
    In the midst of his laughter and glee,
He had softly and suddenly vanished away,
    For the Snark *was* a Boojum, you see.

Charles was not quite sixty-six when he died. He gave up photography in 1880, and laid aside the enchanting excitement of devising unique amusements for little girls, and the satisfaction of devising fiendishly ingenious double acrostics. His last years were spent, peacefully and seriously, in pondering on graver and more fundamental questions.

*

Like Carroll, Edward Lear was an artist as well as an inspired creator of nonsense, always logical in the case of Carroll, never in that of Lear. But just as Carroll was a brilliant photographer, so Lear was a dedicated painter whose work stands out among the myriad other Victorian landscapists. Both had practical, hard-working, no-nonsense professions.

Lear's background could hardly have been more different from Carroll's. Instead of the comfort and stability of Croft Rectory, Lear was the youngest of no fewer than twenty children, several of whom failed to survive childhood. His family had been distinctly prosperous in the fruit trade for several generations, and one of them had been Renter Warden of the Fruiterers' Company. But in the slump following the Napoleonic Wars his father had fallen on very hard times, and had even briefly been in prison for fraud and debt. The spacious family home in Holloway, then a prosperous outpost like Chiswick or Wimbledon, was let to a Jewish family, who 'always opened the windows in thunderstorms – for the easier entrance of the Messiah, but to greater spoiling of the furniture'. The large family split up; the elder ones had to fend for themselves, and Edward, at the age of four, was handed over to his eldest sister Ann to be looked after. She was twenty-one years older than him, and evidently a warm, humorous and good-natured person. They loved each other dearly. Later, the family got back their old home, but they lived a great deal more frugally than before, and Edward's mother had nothing more to do with his upbringing. By the sound of it, it was not a happy home, with regular rows and dramas. As a result, Edward for the rest of his life sought to avoid quarrels and arguments, and went out of his way for gentleness and tranquillity. He also suffered on and off from epilepsy, an alarming condition for which there was no clinical treatment at the time. Although he was much protected by his older sisters, he was often ill, and thrown back on his imagination.

It was not a happy childhood, but Edward's powers of invention and fantasy may well have developed in it more fully than they would have otherwise. Certainly, a combination of humour and real sadness seems to have been the outcome. One of his surviving sisters, Sarah, had married and lived near Arundel, and in that neighbourhood Edward met Lord Egremont, and another great patron of Turner, Walter Fawkes. He also met Lord de Tabley, who had founded the British Institution for the Encouragement of British Art. Finding himself at the age of sixteen on the fringe of the artistic world, he resolved to begin to earn his living by painting, especially birds, which were very much in vogue at the time, and by giving drawing lessons wherever he could. He and Ann settled in modest lodgings off Grays Inn Road.

Edward's first large project was in the end beyond his means: it was for a book of paintings of *The Family of Psittacidae*, or Parrots, intended to consist of fourteen folios. Unfortunately, the cost of printing the colours printed to a standard that satisfied him was prohibitive and only twelve were produced. However, among the subscribers that he succeeded in attracting were Lord Stanley, the son and heir of the eighty-year-old Lord Derby. Stanley was President of the Zoological Society, and was soon to become one of the most important figures in his life. At his home at Knowsley, near Liverpool, he had established a private menagerie which was famous throughout Europe, and he invited Lear to come and make drawings of some of the animals.

The house was often full of members of the extended Stanley family, and the extremely hospitable Lord Derby, noticing that the younger members of the party were apt to slip away after dinner instead of keeping him company, inquired the reason. He was told that there was such an amusing young man in the steward's room that they wanted to be where he was. He replied that if he was such good company he must come and eat with the family. Knowsley was run on a much grander scale than most royal households. Every day from June to October the table was laid for forty, except on Mondays, when even larger numbers of neighbours and local officials and other worthies were regularly entertained. Lear had had little or no experience of social life at all, and being thrown in at the deep end at Knowsley, could not know if he was regarded as a guest or an employee.

In the nursery, however, he was as happy as the children who he entertained so well. He started by drawing pictures in old nursery books, but then went on to compose and illustrate rhymes of his own. But he could also feel very lonely when the children had gone to bed, and he was surrounded by people with many of whom he had nothing in common at all. As in his own childhood, and often again in his later life, when the fun was over, a great melancholy would descend upon him. But he was at Knowsley a great deal between 1832 and 1837, and over a hundred of his drawings remain in the library there to this day. Then a further complication set in. He had suffered from asthma and bronchitis as a child, and now the endless damp of Lancashire made things worse. He needed somewhere warm and dry. Lord Stanley (by this time Derby) kindly offered to pay for him to winter in Rome, where he could recover his health and study painting seriously. Lear wrote to his sister, 'I have the kindest lot of friends any man ever had.'

Pausing, and drawing, in Luxembourg, Frankfurt and among the castles of Bavaria, roaming round the lakes at Lugano and Como, and stopping in Florence since there were rumours of the plague at Rome, Edward finally reached Rome in December. He soon found commissions among the large English colony; art was in the air and artists were accepted as normal beings; it was all very unlike London. He spent most of the next five years in Italy, generally returning to England in August, a notoriously unhealthy month in Rome. In 1845, always in need of earning more money, he had the idea of publishing the 'nonsenses' that had so delighted the children at Knowsley. They were a tremendous success, the reason being that until that time children's books had been serious, improving and often dauntingly dull. Frivolity and jokes had been thought to be quite unsuitable material for children, who apart from being seen and not heard, were there to learn, and not to be amused. Lear did not invent the limerick, but he composed hundreds of them, though for some reason he was tied down by the habit of repeating the first line in the last, which sounds curiously flat to modern ears. Be that as it may, *A Book of Nonsense* was a huge success, although published anonymously, as was much else at the time. Edward then decided to complete a more serious, and much more lavish, book describing his travels in the Abruzzi Mountains. It was beautifully illustrated, and cost no less than four guineas. One far-reaching result was that a copy came into the hands of Queen Victoria, herself a distinctly accomplished artist. In July 1846 she summoned Lear to Osborne, and he began to give her a series of twelve painting lessons. The Queen enjoyed showing her treasures to those considered worthy, and Lear was so delighted by the contents of one showcase that he exclaimed exuberantly 'Oh, where *did* you get all these beautiful things?' 'I inherited them, Mr Lear,' was the reply. Few artists are entirely conventional, but it is doubtful if any other monarch had an instructor quite like Edward Lear.

For the next twenty years he led a wandering life in the Mediterranean: as well as Italy, he went travelling and painting in

Corfu, Palestine and Egypt, where he was enchanted by the light and the birds and the temples. 'But some things in the world *are* NOT pleasant, to wit beetles in your hair; the odoriferous nature of respected domestics; fleas; and the gulpyroarygroanery of camels.' His motive for all these wanderings was partly that it was cheaper to live in the Mediterranean than in England, partly that it was warmer. But the cheapness was more than offset by the expense of getting there, and the advantages had to be set against the fact that he was always having to persuade his friends, and *their* friends, to buy his pictures, often before they were finished. On top of that, his moments of delight in the splendid and then little known landscapes that he discovered alternated with a dreadful loneliness. He occasionally came back to England for short visits, and on one of these went to see the Tennysons at Farringford in the Isle of Wight. He felt happier there than elsewhere, but was sad to find the poet's wife Emily tired and ill, seemingly from wearing herself out ministering to her husband. 'I should think,' he wrote to his friend Chichester Fortescue, 'computing moderately, that 15 angels, several hundreds of ordinary women, many philosophers, a heap of truly wise and kind mothers, 3 or 4 minor prophets, & a lot of doctors and schoolmistresses, might all be boiled down, and yet their continued essence fall short of what Emily Tennyson really is.'

This extract is a good example of Edward's method of escaping from sorrows by writing light-hearted letters and dashing off light-hearted drawings for the amusement of friends young and old. On this occasion, when he left Farringford, a heavy post-happiness depression set in, and in another characteristic letter to Fortescue he wrote 'I am going little but dimly walking on along the dusty twilight lanes of incomprehensible life. I wish you were married. I wish I were an egg & was going to be hatched.' From time to time he contemplated marriage (there were probably several spinsters, such as Augusta Bethell, the daughter of the Lord Chancellor Westbury, who would cheerfully have taken him on) but it would have involved disclosing his epilepsy, and this might have led to his being first accepted and then rejected. Consequently, he could never bring himself to ask. As his biographer puts it, passion did not much come into it. 'His ideal was a gentle companion, who would look after him in a rounded, contented kind of way.' One of his most delightful nonsense poems, on the *Yonghy-Bonghy-Bó*, seems to touch on this.

'Lady Jingly! Lady Jingly!
Sitting where the pumpkins blow.
Will you come and be my wife?',
Said the Yonghy-Bonghy-Bó.
'I am tired of living singly,
On this coast so wild and shingly,
I'm aweary of my life;
If you'll come and be my wife,
Quite serene would be my life',
Said the Yonghy-Bonghy-Bó,
Said the Yonghy-Bonghy-Bó.

At one point Lear had a truly eccentric, and characteristic, adventure in a railway carriage, where a father who was reading *A Book of Nonsense* to his children, explained to them that the author was really Lord Derby. 'He did not choose to publish it openly; but if you transpose the letters LEAR, they make EDWARD EARL.' Lear at this point could not help chipping in that he had reason to know that Edward Lear was indeed the author and illustrator. 'And I,' said the other, 'have good reason to know Sir that you are wholly mistaken. *There is no such person as Edward Lear.*' 'But there is,' replied Lear. 'I am the man, and I wrote the book!' He then took off his hat and showed them his name and address printed on the band inside; also one of his cards, and a marked handkerchief, 'on which amazement devoured those benighted individuals & I left them to gnash their teeth in trouble and tumult'.

The year of 1845 had been wonderful for him. He had published a successful book of nonsense, he had become drawing master to the Queen, he had brought out a travel book, a volume of landscape drawings and one of natural history illustrations for Lord Derby. These publications covered the whole spectrum of his working life but they yielded only £100 profit.

He spent the next few years mostly in various parts of the Mediterranean, Italy, Egypt, where the bird and plant life inspired many of his most delightful nonsense drawings, as well as landscapes bathed in the most perfect light he had ever known; Greece, and Corfu, where he felt the need of company, and complained that 'there was nobody in this rustymustyfustydustybustycrusty Corfu' with whom he could discuss his work, or indeed anything else; Palestine in 1857-8; Rome again from 1858-60, with one winter spent rather surprisingly at the Oatlands Park Hotel, Walton-on-Thames, and another in Corfu again. It was a restless, wandering life, and gave him little satisfaction and much worry, since he seemed quite unable to sell any of his paintings. His perpetual trouble was a gloomy loneliness, all the more surprising when he had such a large collection of friends who were devoted to him. But he was cut off from them, partly because his health prevented him from settling contentedly in England, and also because of his need to try and earn his living as a peripatetic artist. Usually something turned up to stave off disaster: another commission from one or other of his rich friends, among others Derby, Northbrook and Lady Waldegrave, who was now married to one of Lear's greatest friends, Chichester Fortescue. But loyal though they were, they sometimes wearied of being asked yet again for payment for a picture which had not always been painted. And the close friendship of Emily Tennyson was an occasional solace, though Lear's visits to Farringford, where they lived in the Isle of Wight, were not easy: Lord Tennyson, as Bertrand Russell recalled many years later, would announce on the one hand that he was in no mood to be disturbed by a mob of curious neighbours and tourists; while soon afterwards he would be complaining that nobody seemed in the least interested in meeting him.

By 1869, Lear had somehow saved enough to buy a plot of land at San Remo, a quiet spot on the Italian Riviera, and to build a decent-sized house on it, with a beautiful view of the sea and a good painting-room. He commented in a light-hearted letter that 'as I have sold no drawings this winter and have no commissions ahead, I shall endeavor to live upon little Figs in summertime and on Worms in winter. I shall have 28 olive trees and a small bed of onions: and a stone terrace, with a gray Parrot and two hedgehogs to walk up and down on it by day and by night ...' He called it the Villa Emily, after his niece in New Zealand. He had also obtained, or thought he had obtained, a restrictive covenant preventing any building that could spoil his view of the sea. But a few years later, to his horror, his neighbour, Miss Kay-Shuttleworth, sold her land to a German who built a four-storey hotel on it, blocking the Villa Emily's view of the sea and wrecking the light for his studio. A more robust and less indecisive character than Edward would have taken strong steps to prevent this breach of covenant, especially as it greatly reduced the value of his own house, on which he had spent all his savings, and which was just about his only tangible asset. Every year, even when he was earning very little (and, of course, he had some profitable years) he had been extremely careful to protect himself against the very real risk of his eyes failing and his being reduced to the near bankruptcy which had overtaken his father and had split up his family in his childhood. As if this danger were not enough, there was the bitter and unexpected blow of being deceived. He, who was the most generous and open-hearted man, who had given innocent pleasure to many thousands, had been effectively swindled by an apparently upright English spinster. Having been advised to ask £7,000 for the villa, he was eventually reduced to accepting £1,600 for it, £400 less than what he had paid for it fourteen years before, even though he had made various improvements, and local property values had increased greatly in the interval.

At this stage, Lear's generous patron Lord Northbrook, one of the various ennobled banking Barings, had been made Viceroy of India, and invited Lear to go out to India and live at his expense for six months; and, obviously, to enter a new, exotic and very fruitful field for landscape painting. Lear acquired £1,000 worth of advance commissions for work that he would do there, but incredibly flew into a rage about a muddle over his luggage with the customs authorities at Suez, and cancelled his trip. Luckily, however, he set out in the following October, and when they reached Bombay Lear 'felt nearly mad from sheer beauty and wonder of foliage! O new palms!!! O flowers!! O creatures!! O beasts!! Colours, and costumes, and myriadisms of impossible picturesqueness!!! These hours are worth what you will.' Naturally, a lot of travelling had been arranged for him, which was even more tiring then than it would be now. His mood swings were abrupt. One moment he would be raving about the colour and beauty of the country; the next he would be crushed by the hurry and movement. Calcutta, Darjeeling, Kinchinjunga came and went; and at Alahabad he had the pleasure of discovering that his poetry had got there before him. He was drawing an owl to amuse a child, when another child called out 'O please draw a pussy cat too! Because you know they went to sea in a boat, with plenty of honey and money wrapped up in a £5 note!' On enquiry, he found that the whole school she went to had been taught 'that remarkable poem!'

Like others, Lear was swept off his feet by the Taj Mahal and the surrounding gardens, with 'innumerable flights of bright green parrots, flitting across like live Emeralds', and many other birds and squirrels. At Delhi, he proceeded to make 'Delhineations of the

Delhicate architecture as is all impressed on my mind as inDelhibly as the Delhiterious quality of the water of that city.' And in Poona he wrote the following little poem:

> She sat upon her Dobie,
>   To watch the Evening Star,
> And all the Punkahs as they passed
>   Cried 'My! how fair you are!'
>
> Around her bower, with quivering leaves,
>   The tall Kamsamahs grew,
> And Kitmutgars in wild festoons
>   Hung down from Tchokis blue ...
>
> Beware, ye Fair! Ye Fair, beware!
>   Nor sit out late at night –
> Lest horrid Cummerbunds should come,
>   And swallow you outright.

A faint echo, perhaps, conscious or otherwise, of that other poem that had appeared from the other great nonsense rhymer, two years earlier.

> Beware the Jabberwock, my son!
>   The jaws that bite, the claws that catch!
> Beware the jubjub bird, and shun
>   The frumious Bandersnatch!

Lear went on south to Madras and Colombo, then by sea up to Bombay, and so home. The trip certainly inspired some of his happiest self-portraits, often somewhat precariously mounted on the back of an elephant, and as always, depicting himself with a body the shape of an orange, on legs like matchsticks, with his pince-nez floating free, at some distance from his nose, and his arms spread out like the wings of some improbable insect.

Somehow, he found the money to build a new villa, this time called the Villa Tennyson, and built as a replica of the Villa Emily, in order to avoid confusing his cat, Foss. The names of the two houses clearly underlined his loyalty and gratitude to the Tennysons. But his troubles were far from over. His faithful Corfiot servant Giorgio, who had looked after him for thirty years and accompanied him even as far as India, died, and Georgio's good-for-nothing sons robbed him and generally made themselves a nuisance. The one woman who he had most wanted to marry, Augusta ('Gussie') Bethell, daughter of the Lord Chancellor Westbury, had, thanks to Edward's chronic indecision, waited for him until her father died before marrying an older man, an invalid, who she knew her father would not have tolerated. But she was now widowed, and in 1883 she came out to visit him at the Villa Tennyson. Once again, some unfathomable mixture of inhibitions held him back from asking her to marry him. He was only sixty-two, but felt that he was 'so dam' old'. His epilepsy was now much less of a problem, but perhaps there was some kind of suppressed homosexual hang-up that had always prevented him from committing himself to her. For whatever reason, Lear, like Lewis Carroll, had never managed to arrive at normal relations with a woman. His health continued to deteriorate, bronchitis followed pleurisy, yet near the very end there were rays of light in his gloom. In 1886, Ruskin wrote in the *Pall Mall Magazine* that he 'did not know of any author to whom I am half so grateful, for my idle self, as Edward Lear. I shall put him first, of *my* hundred authors.'

The end came in January 1888, after another visit from the faithful Gussie, who if he had felt braver, could have nursed him comfortably through his last months, and could perhaps have prolonged them peacefully for him. He was alone except for a new servant, Giuseppe

Orsini, who recorded his last words: 'My good Giuseppe, you will render me a sacred service in telling my friends and relations that my last thought was for them, especially the Judge (Lushington), Lord Northbrook and Lord Carlingford. I cannot find words sufficient to thank my good friends for the good they have always done me. I did not answer their letters because I could not write, as no sooner did I take a pen in my hand than I felt as if I were dying.'

His very perceptive and sympathetic biographer, Vivien Noakes, summed up his nature and put it into as sharp a focus as is possible with her comment that 'perhaps even he knew that from this very perception of sadness had grown a compassion, an understanding, and a pity for man's suffering, and it was this compassion that made him the loved and loving man he was.'

It could hardly be expected that anyone as idiosyncratic as Edward Lear should have had followers, or that his wayward imagination could have produced any heirs. Yet there is a sense in which a very different creator of a certain amount of nonsense a hundred years later can be described as continuing the genre which he founded.

John Lennon, like Lear, came from a broken home, but there any similarity of context ceases. Lennon's home in war-damaged Liverpool was rough and uncultivated, but not exactly deprived. He was short-sighted, like Lear, and refused in his youth to wear glasses, which he considered disfiguring and unmanly. His method of dealing with short sight consisted of ignoring everything that he couldn't see, and to compensate for this he needed to make himself the centre of attention, as when, in his school days, he set fire to a massive Guy Fawkes bonfire on 4 November. Above all, he needed a gang to lead. His aggressiveness was very far removed from Lear's civilised, gentle amiability; in fact their only resemblance lay in the remarkable talent Lennon had, before he slumped into a swamp of drugs, for inventing nonsense words and rhymes. 'A monk, a mink, a minibus, a marmalaydy moon' is a line that sticks in the mind. This probably derived as much from dyslexia as from natural imagination, but it did lead to some very charming, Learish lines of a vaguely surrealist but above all anarchic kind. His greatest triumph was his even-handed description of the result of the General Election of 1964.

Azue orl gnome, Harassed Wilsod won the General Erection, with a very small marjorie over the Torchies. Thus pudding the Laboring Party back into powell after a large abcess. This he could not have done withoutspan the barking of the Trade Onions, heady by Frank Cunnings (who noun has a SAFE SEAT in Nuneating thank you ...)

Sir Alice Doubtless-Whom was – quote – 'bitherly dithapointed' but managed to keep smirking on his 500,000 acre estate in Scotland with a bit of fishing and that.

The Torchies (now in apperition) have still the capable qualities of such disable men as Rabbit Bunloaf and the very late Harrods McMillion. What, you arsk, happened to Answerme Enos (ex Prim Minicar) after that Suez pudding, peaple are saying. Well, I don't know.

We must not forget the great roles played out by Huge Foot and Dingie in capturing a vote or tomb ... We must not forget Mr Caravans loving smile on Budgie Day as he raised the price of the Old Age Pests. We must not forget Mr Caravans lovely smile when he raised the price of the MPs (Mentals of Parliament) wagers also. We must not forget Joke Grimmace (LIB).

It seems unlikely, though not impossible, that Lennon had read any of Lear's rhymes; but there is a similar streak of zany but imaginative humour in both.

10

Victoria Woodhull Martin

(1838–1927)

Victoria Woodhull was a major feminist pioneer in the United States in the period immediately following the Civil War, a time when national wounds had to be healed, and innumerable ways of creating a satisfactory new world were emerging. She was much more than a feminist pioneer, and since this book is concerned with British eccentrics, she is included on the grounds of her eventual marriage in 1883 to an English banker, John Biddulph Martin, and her life in England until her death, in her ninetieth year, in 1927. Her entire career has been covered in books published in America, but in England she is almost unknown.

Her early days were unpromising. Her father, Buck Claflin, was an enterprising but unreliable entrepreneur who tried his hand at logging on the Susquehanna, unscrupulous horse-trading and speculations of various kinds. After his marriage, he prospered for a time, until the recession of 1837 destroyed the rickety fortune that he had put together, and he went to pieces. Her mother was superstitious, religious and much given to spiritualism. Victoria was named after the Queen, and showed unusual intelligence in her fitful school days, and apparently developed an astonishing memory: she could allegedly read through a page and then repeat it by heart.

She later invented, and reinvented, various accounts of her childhood, but it seems clear that it was in order to escape from an eternal round of household drudgery that she decided to marry, at the age of fifteen, a man not unlike her unreliable father. Like many others at the time, Canning Woodhull called himself a doctor, on the strength of eight months' medical study and a brief apprenticeship. He proved to be a total liability, almost always drunk, even while delivering their son, Byron, who turned out to be mentally handicapped. In 1853 they moved to San Francisco, where largely thanks to her extraordinary memory, Victoria landed a part on the stage, and for six weeks earned the highly satisfactory sum of $52 a week. But she decided at once that she needed wider audiences than could be found in theatres. Spiritualism and mesmerism were much in fashion, and whether truthfully or not, Victoria later described what happened when Byron contracted scarlet fever, from which her youngest sister had died earlier, and actually appeared to be already dead himself:

Without knowing what I did, I ripped my clothes open and clasped Byron to my breast with all my strength. As I did so, the ceiling of the room disappeared from my view, and the form of the Saviour descended. I stood fixed, with Byron thus clasped in my arms, for seven hours. When I returned to consciousness and released him from my arms he was not only restored to life, but the disease was gone.

She had other successes as a faith healer. After the birth of another child, called Zula after a black tulip then in fashion, Victoria decided that she could endure her husband's perpetual drunkenness no longer and divorced him. Her sister, Tennessee, who was to play a vital part in her career, was meanwhile being exploited by her parents as a rather bogus fortune teller, her unscrupulous father netting $50 or even $100 a day from her performances. Much worse was to follow. Buck Claflin decided to extend Tennessee's services to the medical field, and after launching a harmless medicine called Miss Tennessee's Magnetio Life Elixir for Beautifying the Complexion and Cleansing the Blood, he thought he could get away with anything. He rented a small hotel near Pittsburgh, and converted it into an infirmary for cancer patients, with Tennessee administering placebos. However, when one of the patients died, she was indicted for manslaughter and had to flee from the state.

Victoria meanwhile seems to have developed, anyway in theory, a revulsion against all this fraud, going so far as to maintain that she would rather go to the stake than practice a deceit. She stitched onto the sleeves of all her dresses the words of Psalm 120: 'Deliver my soul O Lord from lying lips and from a deceitful tongue.' By 1864 she was in St Louis; she was consulted as a 'spiritualistic physician' by a Union officer, Colonel James Harvey Blood, lately back from the Civil War, who was busy serving as secretary of the St Louis Society of Spiritualists, as well as Auditor of St Louis and President of the St Louis Railroad. Swept off his feet, he abandoned his wife and moved with Victoria to Dayton, Ohio, where he went through a form of marriage with her about which they made various contradictory statements in later life: that they were later divorced, that their marriage had been annulled, that they had remarried in Chicago (where a great fire had conveniently destroyed the civil records in 1871).

It was time for Victoria's professional life to take a new turn. State authorities had tightened up medical standards, and stray spiritualists were no longer legally free to choose their own methods. In the spring of 1868, Victoria and Tennessee headed for New York, possibly with their sights trained on the railroad king Cornelius Vanderbilt, known as The Commodore, the richest man in America, who was well known to have a soft spot for clairvoyants (especially after the death of his youngest and favourite son from tuberculosis at the age of twenty-four) and a sharp eye for female beauty, which the sisters undoubtedly possessed. They had also had cards printed, proclaiming themselves as clairvoyants, and Victoria naturally later claimed that they had been guided to Vanderbilt's 'fatherly care and kindness' by some helpful spirit hand. Vanderbilt immediately recognised them as 'ladies of resource', especially after they established themselves only a few doors from his office on West 4th Street. He often joined them for seances, and in the case of Tennie (as Tennessee was sometimes known), almost certainly for something more intimate. To quote Victoria's somewhat wooden biography by Lois Beachy Underhill, 'the sisters projected good breeding and sexual availability, gentility and sensuality ... always totally feminine, they understood the masculine psyche of the day, with a 'wonderful magnetism' of their own. ... Tennie developed the style of a natural, easygoing courtesan, impetuous, uninhibited, seemingly shallow. Victoria was loftier, more idealistic. She needed a high-minded rationalisation to justify her unconventional sexual behaviour.'

Vanderbilt had a wife who he had committed to a lunatic asylum because she had refused to move from Staten Island to Manhattan. She died in August 1868, a few months after the arrival of the sisters in New York. He immediately proposed marriage to Tennessee, who turned him down, perhaps thinking that her hold over him would be greater as a result. Very imaginatively, she dug into her savings and spent no less than $2,000 on a present for the Commodore's seventy-fifth birthday. It was an oil painting called 'Aurora', of a life-size Venus trailing wisps of gauze. But not surprisingly, Vanderbilt's son William was less than enthusiastic about his ancient father's entanglement, and produced a distant cousin, who was a few years older than Tennie. Vanderbilt eloped with her to Canada, and they were married the following August.

The sisters now wisely played their depleted cards with great skill, realising that if Vanderbilt could be made to feel that he owed them a favour, their position might be far stronger than before. Victoria now became convinced that women's suffrage was to be the stage on which her colossal histrionic powers should be deployed. Two years earlier, an amendment to the Kansas state constitution had proposed full voting rights for women and blacks. National leaders had recommended that only the blacks, and male blacks at that, should be enfranchised. Enraged, the women's champions had proclaimed that black men were intellectually inferior to white women; abolitionists fought back, and the result was, predictably, that neither women nor blacks got the vote. By her quiet and intelligent speeches at the Washington convention Victoria made a small name for herself as 'the coming woman', and the *New York World* announced that she was 'to rise to a very conspicuous position ... destined to act a part in the coming conflicts and reforms'.

Still she was not in a hurry. Realising that what she needed in order to publicise herself and her views was money in great quantities, Victoria returned to New York and in September made a large amount in the 'great bear gold panic' on Wall Street, the result of Jay Gould's wild attempt to corner gold. Vanderbilt described her as 'a bold operator', a compliment which she noted down for her autobiography. At this stage William Vanderbilt tried to remove them from the scene by offering them a free trip to Europe for a year. Instead, Victoria explained to Cornelius that her spirit guide was propelling her in the direction of Wall Street. Amused, he gave the sister a cheque for $7,000, and the word soon got around that he was behind their venture, which was the foundation of Woodhull, Claflin & Co., stockbrokers. Victoria's strategy was to prove, with a large slice of help from Vanderbilt, that 'a female invasion of the masculine precincts of finance' would show that women were as good as men, and that *all* women benefited by the example of one woman competing successfully in male territory. Besides investing, the sisters used all their skills to win over press interviewers, which in turn drummed up further business. 'Queens of Finance', and 'Bewitching Brokers' were two of the headlines which they inspired. According to another note tucked away by Victoria for her memoirs, no less a figure than Walt Whitman described them as 'two great children of nature in this swarming vortex of life ... You have given an object lesson to the whole world ... You are a prophecy of the future'.

At first the chorus of admirers was male. But before long the joint founder of a suffragist newspaper, *The Revolution*, came to interview Tennessee, and in due course reported that 'the new firm, Mesdames Woodhull & Claflin, who have made such a sensation in Wall Street, will stimulate the whole future of women by their efforts and example. They are full of pluck, energy and enterprise ... moreover, they "know what they are about", and are calculated to inspire confidence by the sound sense, judgement and clear-sightedness they show in financial matters.' This was no more than tame propaganda, but it was not disbelieved. The sisters were now doing business, which even sometimes overlapped, for both the Commodore and his arch-rival Jay Gould. According to Gould, he paid them $1,000 a day in commission 'through quite a spell'. Nor was business confined to office hours. What were described as 'very popular after-business levees', that is to say more or less open house, were skillfully organised by the sisters in smart rooms at the Astor House Hotel. Among those who attended were President Grant's old chief of staff, the presidents of the Western Union Co., the Home Fire Insurance Co., the Continental Bank, and of course, the Vice-President of Union Pacific Railroad, Cornelius Vanderbilt. But there were others closer to the causes that were so dear to Victoria's heart. Albert Brisbane, a Fourierist Reformer from a rich New York family; the Reverend Octavius Brooks Frothingham, and even Josiah Warren, the founder of American philosophical anarchism. The net could hardly have been spread wider.

It was time for a second bombshell, for which the first had cleared the way. At the end of March 1870, Victoria offered herself as a candidate for the presidency of the United States. The fact that women did not have the vote was quite immaterial: indeed, one of her less flamboyant but equally voteless fellow suffragists had stood for Congress four years earlier, and as Victoria put it, 'The blacks were cattle in 1860. A Negro now sits in Jeff Davis's seat in the Senate.' Did not American womanhood deserve something at least equal, if not better? Of course, her motive was to draw attention to herself and to the women's cause across the country. She had about as much chance of being elected as Screaming Lord Sutch at Westminster a century later, but that was not the point.

Simultaneously, most of the company's Wall Street profits were invested in *Woodhull and Claflin's Weekly*, whose sole purpose was to 'support Victoria C. Woodhull for president ... and to advocate suffrage without distinction of sex', though it was soon to cover financial news from Wall Street as well. Victoria's next thunderbolt was to announce in an editorial that there was no need in law to give women the vote: they had it already, since the Constitution nowhere uses the word 'man' but only 'citizen' with regard to the power to vote. She petitioned Congress to pass enabling legislation to confirm her interpretation. Unfortunately, the House Judiciary Committee ruled that women were not in fact citizens, and for the time being that was that. But as a propaganda move, her petition was sensational.

Her next step was to book the Lincoln Hall, the largest in Washington, and to take her case to the people. She held the attention of the packed hall for an hour and a quarter, and two months later, in March 1871, she spoke again at large halls in New York, Philadelphia and Boston. She began to broaden her programme to include not just the suffrage, but a crusade against double-dealing and misleading prospectuses in business, scandals in the property and insurance worlds, and other grievances. Needless to say, her success attracted hostility, among others from the best known woman in the States, Harriet Beecher Stowe. (President Lincoln, referring to *Uncle Tom's Cabin*, had said on being introduced to her, 'So you're the little lady who made the big war.') Stowe opposed the Woodhull movement, which included setting up a new political party, since neither of the others would support her claims, some of which opposed the most powerful vested interests of the day. Stowe objected, in the first place, to Victoria's domestic arrangements in New York, which were indeed eccentric in the extreme. They were revealed to an astonished public when Victoria's mother, who by this time seems to have become erratic and possibly deranged, brought a court case against her 'son-in-law' Col. Blood, who turned out to have, almost certainly, another wife, abandoned but not divorced. Mrs Claflin claimed that Blood had threatened her life several times, and had alienated both her daughters from her. It then transpired that Victoria's house was lived in not only by herself and Blood and Tennessee and their mother and father, but also the wretched Dr Woodhull (who Victoria explained was 'sick, ailing and incapable of self-support') and their son Byron, not to mention another sister of Victoria's, Mary Sparr, her second husband and four children.

All this scandal caused a sensation on a predictable scale, and Victoria ended by declaring that she advocated free love 'in the highest and purest sense as the only cure for the immorality, the deep damnation by which men corrupt and disfigure God's most holy institution of sexual relations'. Although this perhaps begged more questions than it answered, she could at least claim to be acting from principle – unlike a man who she proceeded to pillory, not for his immorality but his hypocrisy. 'I know of one man,' she declared, 'a public teacher of eminence who lives in concubinage with the wife of another public teacher of almost equal eminence.'

The other 'public teacher' was an apparently irresistible poet, and ghost writer, called Theodore Tilton, who had been having affairs with various women in the suffrage movement, and Victoria now enthusiastically joined their number. Tilton's wife was indeed one of the many concubines of Henry Ward Beecher, a famous preacher at Plymouth Church and none other than the brother of Harriet

Beecher Stowe. A man who attended suffragist meetings told Victoria that he was 'reliably informed that Mr Beecher preaches to at least twenty of his mistresses every Sunday'. How any of those involved in this cat's cradle of sex and sermons, all covered by a heavy coating of hypocrisy, managed to keep their sanity, remains a mystery. But Victoria, who was at least completely open about her theories and her activities, summed up her own attitude in the *Weekly*, writing that 'Every great man of Mr Beecher's type has had, in the past, and will ever have the need for, and the right to, the loving manifestations of many women, and when the public graduates out of the ignorance and prejudice of its childhood, it will recognise this necessity and its own injustice.' On a higher note, she also wrote an introduction to a new edition of Goethe's *Elective Affinities*, in an attempt to persuade Beecher to come off the fence and proclaim in public what they had both practised in private.

In the summer of 1871, however, Victoria cooled down on free love, and turned her thoughts to forming a new political party, declaring that the Republican Party was too corrupt ever to produce another President. In a letter in the *Weekly*, addressed to herself, she soliloquises as follows:

> A number of your fellow-citizens, both men and women, have formed themselves into a committee, borrowing your name, and calling itself the Victoria League. Our object is to form a new national political organisation, composed of the progressive elements in the existing Republican and Democratic parties ... to be called the Equal Rights Party.

She followed this with an invitation to herself to become the standard-bearer of the party, and then nominated herself as its candidate for President, offering herself the party's great esteem, and 'the cheerful prescience of victory'. She also arranged for hints to be dropped that Vanderbilt was the party's President. Looking around for more tangible support, she succeeded in getting herself made, rather to her surprise, president of the Spiritualists' movement. She explained this by claiming that she had felt called upon by 'the higher powers' to enact a great role, 'a swelling and overmastering desire for an immense usefulness to my suffering fellow-beings'.

The first manifestation of this call was unsuccessful. Victoria and a party of other women attempted to cast their votes in the New York City election in November, but were turned away by the stony-hearted inspector of the poll. Though a failure, this effort did greatly increase the public demand for Victoria's lectures, now made very necessary by the fact that she had spent most of the large earnings that the sisters had made on Wall Street. Shrewdly reverting to the subject of free love, she addressed a crowd of 3,000 people in the Steinway Hall in New York. She had asked Beecher to introduce her on the platform, but his courage failed and he weakly refused. Tilton was an adequate substitute. Her message was that it should be possible to end loveless marriages, like her own, but that she believed that the very highest sexual unions were monogamic, whether 'serially', 'exclusively', or 'experimentally', so long as the motives were 'pure', that is to say entirely genuine and not the result of exploitation, i.e., presumably, prostitution. Her reception in the press was not unfriendly, and she set off on a whistle-stop tour, lecturing in eleven cities in the next thirteen days.

Free love taking a back seat for a while, the next targets in her presidential campaign were the labour reformers. 'A system of society which permits such arbitrary distribution of wealth is a disgrace to Christian civilisation,' she thundered, rather ungratefully turning on her old benefactor Vanderbilt, as well as on Mr Astor (real estate) and Mr Stewart, who was the leading New York retailer. It seems that she did genuinely believe in individual freedom and the idea of making it available to excluded groups; unlike the Marxist doctrine of unavoidable class conflict, as if human beings were mere automata, obediently abiding by imaginary laws. But for a time she adopted a sort of Christian communism, gliding smoothly over the problem of how it was to be put into practice. 'I answer very easily,' she said. 'When a person worth millions dies, instead of leaving his fortune to his children, it must revert to the people.' Precisely what would happen to it then, and who was to make the decisions about distributing it, was not something she explained.

The press were shocked into silence. But Victoria reinforced her point well when she announced in her *Weekly* that 'working people have rights which capital has never respected, and which the *Times*, and other papers conducted in the interests of bond-holders, money-lenders and Republican officials, are determined never shall be recognised.' To her credit, it was a point which she pursued for a time, often in the face of indifference, or of suppression on the part of strong vested interests. If she had stuck to that line, she would have an honourable place among radical politicians. But there were many other things that she wanted as well, which were to lead her to five painful years of disaster.

Victoria also found time care for the wretched Canning Woodhull, who was a morphine addict as well as an alcoholic, and had often maltreated her in the past. Fortunately for her, he died at the age of forty-eight, in 1872, when she was still only thirty-four. A month later came the inaugural convention to establish the Equal Rights Party, which Victoria had organised in the teeth of the usual opposition from older and more staid rivals who had never turned their attention to professional success and the independence, both psychological and financial, that it could bring. Her chief male supporters included both 'Christian Communists' and Christian capitalists, agrarian reformers, spiritualists, as well as Belva Lockwood, the first woman to be allowed to practise at the Supreme Court, and Robert Dale Owen, the son of the great Manchester philanthropic employer and publicist, who had been largely responsible for the Factory Act of 1810. Robert Dale Owen had joined the New Harmony settlement in Indiana at the age of twenty-five, and also served as US Minister in Naples in the 1850s. The Convention's proposed areas of activity were education, suffrage and a series of industrial and social reforms. Although the party never achieved much itself, it may be said to have inspired such later measures as direct taxation, the regulation of monopolies, laws to protect labour, and a civil service based on merit. It was less successful in its advocacy of nationalisation of industries, and the public ownership of land, water and minerals; but a visionary idea for the establishment of a universal government with international arbitration for wars can be regarded as a distant forerunner of the United Nations.

Whatever the priorities of her most able supporters may have been, Victoria was concentrating firmly on her campaign as a candidate for the presidency. She had, however, run out of money, and Col. Blood's plan of issuing bonds, redeemable when the party became victorious, failed to appeal to investors. Victoria unwisely chose as her running mate the Negro leader Frederick Douglass, but none of her previous efforts had been in the direction of black voters and Douglass himself was busy with a convention of his own. Her move therefore fell flat. On top of that, the Grand Opera House in New York, where she had planned to hold her ratification meeting, cancelled her booking, on the grounds of what it called the 'class of people' likely to attend. Further public frustrations and embarrassments followed, nobody would buy the bonds, and she had failed to appreciate how much her support of communism, even a Christian variety, would antagonise those, especially on Wall Street, who had been so captivated when she began operating there.

Worst of all, however, was the major recession that developed in 1873. An intense railway building programme overreached itself, the New York Stock Exchange closed for ten days. Unemployment grew and five years of recession were to follow. Woodhull, Claflin & Co. went under, and many of the suffragists lost faith in Victoria: one of them removed much of her credibility by stating that her views on free love opened the door to any 'weak or vicious soul who now moves carelessly from flower to flower sucking poisonous sweets', which if not felicitously expressed contained more than a grain of truth. Nobody would rent her a house. Eventually, she and her children were reduced to sleeping in her office, and a cheaper office at that. She appeared in court for non-payment of debts; both Tilton and Belva Lockwood went off to support other candidates; and she had to suspend publication of her beloved *Weekly*, so that she could not even communicate with any supporters who might still be faithful.

In desperation, all Victoria could think of to revive interest in the *Weekly* was to print a lurid and more detailed exposure of the Beecher/Tilton scandal. It was far from free of hypocrisy, since at the same time she announced her view that the institution of marriage 'has outlived its day of usefulness ... the most intelligent and virtuous of our citizens ... only submit to it from the dread of a sham public opinion.' Her attack was maliciously timed to coincide with the silver jubilee of Beecher's arrival at the Plymouth Church. Even if it were justified in the way that she claimed, Victoria should have had the sense to realise that by turning the *Weekly* into a scandal sheet, she was forfeiting any right to be taken seriously in her general political crusade. But for the time being, her judgement, often so shrewd in the past, had completely deserted her in the overwhelming crisis that she faced.

An unpopular, self-appointed guardian of the public morals by the name of Comstock now succeeded in getting a warrant for the arrest of Victoria and her colleagues on the charge of sending obscene material through the mail. By now the knives were well and truly out and Victoria's supporters were advised that if they accepted the bail that was offered them, they would immediately be rearrested on other charges, which in due course happened, after the police had ransacked the *Weekly* offices. The tide had turned viciously against the sisters, but new well-wishers came forward, and while on bail Victoria disguised herself as an elderly Quaker woman and succeeded in taking the stage at a mass meeting at the Cooper Institute which she had announced earlier, but at which the police had decided that she should not be allowed to appear. She was allowed to make a violent speech, uninterrupted, and at the end of it held out her wrists as if to be handcuffed.

At one stage Victoria collapsed under the stress and remained unconscious on and off for five days before making a startling recovery. In June 1873 she stood trial for obscenity, but was eventually found not guilty, and public opinion swayed back in her favour. However, the more conventional element in the suffrage movement did not want to be publicly identified with her, because they knew how many of their supporters would be antagonised by wholehearted support of free love and any form of communism. Victoria came back fighting with a series of bold speeches about the sexual emancipation of women, which she declared was, among other things, the 'sublime mission of spiritualism'. She was still able to attract passionate supporters, but so wild had her speeches become, both politically and in sexual frankness, that she seemed to have lost any real sense of her own interest, or of how best to pursue her original objectives, for which there was in theory so much support. Eventually, a certain Dr Treat, who had for a time been her fervent admirer, and who she had unwisely employed on the *Weekly*, also turned against her and published a series of pamphlets accusing her of being a prostitute, and 'advocating harlotry'. He also stated that she had never in fact herself written any of the stirring articles and editorials that had appeared over her name. Furthermore, he invited her to disclose her own personal sexual history, just as she had disclosed that of Dr Beecher.

One gets the feeling that Victoria was now wearying of this perpetual treadmill of scandal. In any case, instead of accepting Dr Treat's invitation, she left for a visit to Paris for several months in 1874, and the next year, after yet another lecture tour, she went down with pleurisy and spent several months recuperating in bed. Treat was eventually sued by Blood for libel, but was released on bail, and in fact died before the case came to court. If only she had abandoned the field of sex promotion and the world of spiritualism, she would, no doubt, have gone further in the respectable sector of the suffrage movement, instead of being abandoned by those who had at first been her enthusiastic allies. Nobody would deny the genuine evidence which supports some of the claims of spiritualism, but in that era it seems to have attracted more than the usual number of frauds, charlatans and parasites, against whom Victoria was seldom on her guard, largely because she was so much occupied with her own oratorical gifts and powers of attraction.

Slowly, and no doubt wearily, she decided to take refuge in respectability. She closed down the *Weekly*, since it could no longer campaign except through making scandalous claims. She fell out with Blood, blaming him for her persecution by Dr Treat, and divorced him.

The atmosphere of New York was changing. The helter-skelter rough and tumble of the period following the Civil War was over, and the more dignified world of Edith Wharton was coming into being, though of course there would always be many exceptions to its decorous calm, as she herself described. Commodore Vanderbilt died in 1877, leaving $100m, almost all of it to his son William. His other children, as well as Tennessee, contested the will. There is considerable doubt about what happened next. It is claimed by some that William Vanderbilt gave the sisters $100,000 to leave the country before the hearing of the suit to set aside the will, on the grounds that the Commodore had not been of sound mind when he had made it. If so, both sides would, no doubt, have preferred to keep it quiet, and no records have survived. But for whatever reason, the sisters found themselves able to emigrate to London in August 1877, and to invent for themselves a completely new existence.

They set up house in some style at 45 Warwick Road in Earl's Court. Victoria embarked on a lecture tour ending at St James's Hall in London, where the audience included John Biddulph Martin, a family partner in Martin's Bank. He had recently lost a much loved sister Penelope, who had had strong views on the unfairness of the treatment of women by society, and the fact that all professions except teaching were closed to them. He had written in his journal a few months before that 1876 had been 'a very disappointing year. ... Is it possible to become more amiable and happy as one grows older?' Martin had followed Victoria's career in America, but seems to have been unaware of its seamy side, or perhaps indifferent to it. When he saw and heard Victoria speak, he 'vowed he would marry her, if she would have him'. There was no contact till August 1879, but he later wrote to a friend that 'she was more alive than anyone I had ever met. ... When you were with her everything became so thrilling, so worthwhile. She wanted people to be happy and she made them happy.' By December 1880 they were engaged. But the Treat pamphlet, describing the Woodhull/Claflin house as a brothel, somehow resurfaced, and Victoria began to deny her past wildly, claiming that she had never advocated free love, or authorised the (innumerable) articles on the subject in her *Weekly*. After two more years, Martin decided that his parents would never consent to the marriage, so he decided to marry first and seek their approval afterwards. Victoria was now 45, and Martin 42, and the marriage took place in a church in Emperor's Gate on 31 October 1883. They were well received on their first visit to the family home at Overbury, near Tewkesbury, but trouble lay ahead.

Victoria had made contact with the London suffragists, but they contacted the formidable Susan Anthony in New York, and the reply came back: 'Let her severely alone. Both sisters are regarded as lewd and indecent. I would advise against any contact.' Henry James, on the other hand, certainly appears to have had Victoria in mind when creating the character of Verena Tarrant in *The Bostonians*. Both her parents died in the next ten years, her father having established himself at the Martins' house at 17 Hyde Park Gate, and her mother at Tennie's grand residence at Doughty House. (Tennie's husband had been created a baronet for his great philanthropic work in establishing Alexandra House, a student hostel in Kensington named as a tribute to the Princess of Wales.)

In 1892 Victoria founded a new magazine, *The Humanitarian*, to propagate 'applied scientific knowledge ... exalting and purifying the entire human race'. It leant heavily on one of Victoria's earlier, discarded gurus, Stephen Pearl Andrews, who had been sent to prison, along with other members of the *Weekly*, at the time of the prosecution for sending obscene material through the post. She launched it in New York under the management of her daughter Zula Maud, as a vehicle for her aims and for her second campaign as a presidential candidate. As before, the whole enterprise was an effort to stake her claim as a leader among nineteenth-century women, and as a protagonist for the genuine causes about which exaggerated claims were made, but which in many cases succeeded in the decades that followed. The records do not show that she was given a single vote.

In fact, some might say that Victoria was not an eccentric at all, but a woman endowed with outstanding powers of oratory, very attractive both in physique and character though apparently humourless, and with a strong tendency to deviousness, manipulation, and when all else failed, downright lying. In her early days she had a shrewd tactical sense, but not surprisingly she went off the rails when confronted with the results of the severe errors of judgement which she made when under pressure. And pressure there certainly was, first through the shortcomings of her parents and her handicapped son, all of whom she steadfastly housed and cared for; and secondly through the hostility of the suffrage champions who disagreed profoundly with many of her other ideas, firmly taking the line that promiscuity brings unhappiness, and that loyalty and a sense of obligation are much to be preferred. Yet there was eccentricity too, in many of her projects, such as her disguise as a Quaker when banned from a meeting.

In England, Victoria's role was more subdued. She interfered mercilessly in the life of her daughter Zula, and rushed off to bring her back from America when there was a possibility that she might get married there. The reason was, in part, a fear that if Zula had children they might be handicapped like Byron, but her possessiveness became neurotic. She secured one of her most surprising victories, or semi-victories, when she sued the British Museum for libel for having on its shelves copies of two collections of American news articles containing lurid details about her life and views. When cross-examined, she denied various improprieties, which at that distance were indeed hard to prove, and in the end she accepted damages of 20 shillings.

In 1896 John Martin died after contracting pleurisy and pneumonia. Victoria inherited his estate of £147,128; she appeared at grand receptions given by the Duchesses of Westminster and Sutherland, and in the gallery of the House of Lords. But five years later she closed down the *Humanitarian*, and began to spend more of her time at Bredon's Norton, a Martin family property of 1,100 acres which her husband had also left her. Curiously enough, the daughter of one of her other sisters, Utica Welles, married Sir Thomas Beecham, though the marriage was not a great success and ended in divorce. She acquired a car, and once received a visit to compare motoring notes from the Prince of Wales, who was staying nearby.

162

After this, her radical aims did not cease, but they were restricted to the Bredon's Norton estate, though she was also the major shareholder in Martin's Bank. She helped to form the Ladies' Automobile Club, and spent time abroad on the Continent. Needless to say, she was active in the country as well. Norton Park, as it was now called, had been empty since the death of Penelope Martin, John's much loved sister. Victoria provided a new organ for the church and presented it with a lectern and a lavish Prayer Book. She provided a new curate with a decent house, with a greenhouse, a rose garden, hens and a Jersey cow. Like much of the rest of rural England, the village was in a primitive state. She had it generally tidied up, installed street lights, caused the postal service to be improved, and campaigned successfully for a village telephone exchange. Very naturally, these improvements were widely resented by villagers who greatly disliked change, even when obviously for the better. Street lights were vandalised, presumably by those who preferred the village to remain in immemorial darkness. After local feeling had cooled, Victoria employed one of her well tried ruses: she imported a journalist to write favourable articles about her activities in the *Tewkesbury Register*.

Later, she founded a Women's School of Gardening and Light Agriculture, which survived until 1914, when it became a victim of wartime priorities. A plan for an agricultural community was less successful, but is said to have taught useful lessons. Her attempt to resurrect the decayed village school on Froebel lines was a disastrous failure, partly because she high-handedly disregarded local opinion, and partly because she mistakenly saw no need to get the approval of the Worcestershire Education Committee, which stated that it was in the dark concerning the Froebel system, in spite of the fact that it had been operating in England for no less than fifty-three years. Victoria had decided to run the school at her own expense until she could obtain a certificate of efficiency from the Board of Education. But although she equipped the school with admirable facilities and a full curriculum, and it was very popular with pupils and parents alike, the Inspector withheld the certificate on the grounds that the premises were inadequate and the standard of discipline and moral training too low.

Gradually she became more cautious, and having had so many rebuffs, less ambitious. She did not join the very active Women's Suffrage Society in Cheltenham, perhaps thinking that as an American it was not for her to do so. But in 1910 she founded a Women's Social Club in the village, which was used, gratefully, by a number of local organisations. She also turned the big house at Norton Park into a successful and fashionable country club, and laid out a golf course, besides providing other facilities. The handsome tithe barn was converted into a concert and lecture hall. A Reading Room (which later became the village post office for over forty years), a Working Men's Club and Village Library followed.

When the war came, Victoria persistently urged the United States Congress to join the Allies, using all her old contacts with the press. Sadly, the war interrupted, for ever as it turned out, a great plan to celebrate the centenary of the Treaty of Ghent, which in 1814 had ended hostilities between Britain and the United States. One of the aims of the celebration was to consolidate Anglo-American relations by means of the Sulgrave Foundation, and to acquire Sulgrave Manor in Northamptonshire, the ancestral home of George Washington's family. Big names had been enlisted on both sides: Theodore Roosevelt, Andrew Carnegie and Elihu Root in America, Lord Crewe, the Secretary of the Pilgrim Trust and the editor of the *Daily Chronicle* in London. Victoria had played a big part in the preliminaries, and various meetings and discussions took place at Bredon's Norton.

After the war, much work was still needed to improve American knowledge and understanding of Britain, and vice versa. It was alleged that in America, people of British extraction were being 'hounded from jobs by cabals of Irish and European immigrants' and were opposed by 'fifty millions of people, representing all the nationalities of Europe who for generations have hated England, and whose representatives in this country still hate her'. Later, Victoria planned to bequeath a large part of her fortune, together with much of the Bredon's Norton estate, to the Sulgrave Institution. Sadly, however, a rift had developed between the British and American halves, and she felt she could not benefit the one without deeply upsetting the other.

In 1922 Victoria was eighty-four years old, and her fighting days were not surprisingly ending, though she still had five years to live. In 1943, a memorial tablet was put up in Tewkesbury Abbey, remembering her as an American citizen 'who devoted herself unsparingly to all that could promote the great cause of Anglo-American friendship', partly triggered off by her daughter Zula giving £5,000 to buy the Abbey Lawn property and two acres of land, to improve the view of the abbey from the main road for ever.

In 1972, Canon J.S. Leatherbarrow inquired bluntly, 'Was she the blatant, licentious careerist of shabby background and amazing good fortune … or was she the angel of light, the social reformer and benefactor of the human race?' A palmist once detected in her 'a naturally hot temper' and 'but little prudence or caution'. There was also an inability to foresee the consequences of her actions, as when she alienated a crucial section of the suffragists in America, and later when she sacked most of the existing staff when she took over at Bredon's Norton, which not unnaturally made her for a time unpopular there. She had few original ideas, but eagerly latched on to whatever novelties appealed to her, such as eugenics. She relied heavily on scriptwriters, passing off what they wrote as her own, and then protesting that things had been written over her name without her consent.

Two of Victoria's other faults were an inability to think things through, and an impatience for action without proper preparation. She saw what she wanted to see, and ended up having persuaded herself that she had achieved greatness, when her actual achievements such as the introduction of women's suffrage first in England and then in America often owed more to others than they did to her. She did a lot, however, for Anglo-American relations in her last active years, and the following statement which she made at the height of her troubles, gives important clues both about her good qualities and her endless fallibility.

So after all I am a very promiscuous free lover. I want the love of you all, promiscuously. It makes no difference who or what you are, old or young, black or white, pagan, Jew or Christian. I want to love you all, and be loved by you all, and I mean to have your love. If you will not give it to me now, these young, for whom I plead, will in after years bless Victoria Woodhull for daring to speak for their salvation.

Perhaps some of them did.

11

Sir Iain Moncreiffe and
Sir Humphry Wakefield

(1919–85 & 1936–)

The genuine eccentricity of Sir Iain Moncreiffe, CVO, DL, QC, FSA, PhD, owed something to the very unusual circumstances of his childhood and upbringing. His father was the younger son of a younger son of the head of a Scottish family whose records go back to the thirteenth century; but in spite of his passion for genealogy Iain would always gently rebuke anyone who referred to an 'old' family. He would point out that all families are of exactly the same age, but some have had more interesting and better known members than others. The Moncreiffes had never been rich, and since Iain's great-grandfather had had no less than eight sons, as well as eight daughters, what money there was was spread thinly.

His father, Lt.-Commander Gerald Moncreiffe, had served briefly in the navy before settling on a coffee plantation in Kenya in 1913, and dying in 1922, when his son was three. Eighteen months later, Rupert, as Iain was first called, had become the proud possessor of a child's solar topee. By this time, a local District Nurse had decided that his mother was too preoccupied with social life to be capable of bringing up her son properly; and one day, Nurse Archibald picked up the topee and told its owner that she was taking it to England. Iain was distraught – until he was told that he might accompany his beloved headgear. Whether Nurse Archibald acted spontaneously, or perhaps more probably, on instructions from Scotland, is unclear. Iain always gave the impression that it was the former: 'When I was kidnapped ...'

He spent the next ten years in the care of his uncle Guy Moncreiffe and his Greek wife, who decided between them that Rupert was a nasty German name, and that he was henceforth to be called Iain. When Sir Guy died in 1934, Iain's widowed grandmother took over. Altogether, there was nothing modern about his formative influences: it was in many ways as if he had been born and brought up into the nineteenth century rather than the twentieth, which goes far to explaining many of his views and standards. Indeed, he sometimes puzzled people by claiming that he had been born in 1887, the year when his grandmother had become a widow, and when her own attitudes to life had perhaps hardened. By the time of his uncle's death Iain had survived various preparatory schools, including one hell-hole in Switzerland, where he later recalled that an eight-year-old girl had been put into a revolving cylindrical clothes-drier by a teacher and told that if she moved it would start up and throw out all her blood; while an equally unfortunate Polish boy had been made to sleep hunched up in a sack, with his sleeves sewn up to cure him of biting his nails. The school owned only two books in English: Freeman Mitford's *Tales of Old Japan*, and a Jacobean romance by D.K. Broster called *The Flight of the Heron*; Iain became for a time better informed on Japanese history than on British, while the other book made the name of Lochiel sacred to him for ever more. So there were compensations as well as horrors. He would spend some of the holidays in the Victoria & Albert Museum, where he continued his studies of Japanese and of much else besides. For a grounding in oriental culture he sought out the jurist Sir Syed Ameer Ali, a friend of his grandmother's, and the author of *The Spirit of Islam*. There were also visits to his grandmother's brother, Sir Kay Muir, and his Bulgarian wife, at Blair Drummond, where on shooting days King Boris, the King of Bulgaria, was apt to be among the guns. His horizons had widened, and were never to contract. He had already been helped at Stowe, where he was taught by a man he later called 'that

168

remarkable falconer-pacifist-huntsman T.H. White', author of *The Sword in the Stone*. White came into the classroom one morning and announced that, G.K. Chesterton having died the day before, 'P.G. Wodehouse is now the greatest living master of the English language.' Iain later took the trouble to establish the fact that the creator of Jeeves, through the marriage of his eighteenth-century forebear Sir Armine Wodehouse, was able to claim Sir Francis Bacon as his ancestral uncle. This led naturally to the question of whether Sir Francis was looking over the shoulder of the great comic genius, at work on the typewriter. Iain's health was still frail, and he often referred to 'weeds like me'.

After a year at Christ Church, where he acquired a great affection for a select but intemperate dining club called Loder's, he found his way to the Guards' Depot at Caterham in the bleak November of 1939. Having naturally set his heart on a commission in the Scots Guards, he found himself being trained by the Coldstream. According to his fellow recruit, and later lifelong friend, Patrick Leigh Fermor, the only relief from the grim greyness of their surroundings was the array of scarlet fire-buckets, suitably adorned with Coldstream battle honours, such as Talavera, Vittoria and Waterloo. Iain quickly mastered not only these, but lesser known victories as well, such as Fuentes de Onoro and Nivelles – together with their dates, the weather, the names of the commanders on both sides, who had red hair, which one had a limp. ... His fascination with the leading personalities of the past was already highly developed, and he would take endless pains to bring them to life in his own mind, and then to pass them on to whoever might (or, just occasionally, might not) be interested.

There followed several years of tough regimental soldiering, in spite of his very shaky health, which dated from two attacks of malaria in his early childhood in Kenya. After a School Marathon at Stowe, he had been obliged to stay in bed for the rest of the term. But he became a past master at disguising this frailty, and would have done anything to avoid being left behind by his beloved battalion. On one occasion, in 1941, Iain concealed his weakness so effectively that he was sent on a 'toughening up' course, which he reluctantly decided would finish his military career for good. But to avoid suspicion he hit on the ingenious idea of sending his soldier servant, Guardsman Alex Fraser, to take his place on the course. Nobody noticed the impersonation, and the fact that the guardsman had been willing to replace him is telling evidence of his ability to get on with all ranks, whether military or social. Later, he joined a quite unusual number of London clubs, and other societies of a more learned kind. But he claimed that sometimes he felt that he preferred the company of the hall porters to that of the members. So much for the accusations of any unpleasant form of snobbery.

Iain's fighting career eventually culminated in the battle of Monte Camino, where heavy German shell fire dislodged a large fragment of the mountainside and sent it crashing into Iain's spine, damaging his back permanently, though not visibly. He did not limp or stoop, but was regularly in considerable pain, for which he sought relief ever after in regular and copious draughts of whisky, and an occasional noggin (a favourite term) of vodka in his breakfast orange juice. Although this sometimes led to unbridled words (rather than deeds) it did not prevent him from continuing his omnivorous studies into the characters of history, and more particularly into their antecedents and ramifications. First, however, being no longer fit for battle, he was seconded as ADC to the GOCinC, Scottish Command, and then as Military Liaison Officer for Norway to the Naval Commander-in-Chief at Rosyth. When the war was over, he was sent as military attache and private secretary to Sir Maurice Peterson in Moscow, a post which led, years later, to an invitation from his friend Sir Fitzroy Maclean to join him and his guest the Soviet Ambassador for lunch at White's Club in London. Iain then considered it his duty to introduce his fellow guest to the blameless hall porter, a courteous Irishman, and to say to the Ambassador: 'I'd like you to meet our friend here. As you're a member of the KGB and he's a member of the IRA, I think you'll find you have a lot in common.' This is an excellent example of the kind of 'tease', inflicted in a deadpan fashion, often on a complete stranger, which occasionally caused massive offence. But there was a childlike innocence about it which led to its being laughed off and forgiven much more often than might have been expected.

Back in England, Iain soon married Diana, the Countess of Erroll in her own right, Hereditary Lord High Constable of Scotland, Senior Great Officer of the Royal Household in Scotland and Chief of the Clan Hay. Like Iain she was an orphan with a Kenyan background, since her father (who she hardly knew) had been murdered there five years earlier. Iain's attitude to her was acutely romantic and chivalrous, and since he was far better versed than her in the history of Scotland, his great aim was to see that she carried out her role as effectively, positively and gloriously as possible. They settled down at first in Edinburgh, but before long moved to Easter Moncreiffe, a charming and manageable dower house (as it would be called in England), not far from Perth, and only a mile or two from Moncreiffe House, where the then head of the family lived. This was Sir David Moncreiffe, a slightly younger but senior cousin of Iain's, who had also been a brother officer in the war. Tragically, the big house, with its owner inside, went up in flames in 1957, leaving Iain quite unexpectedly as head of the family and the clan. Historical associations were always near the surface of life at Easter Moncreiffe and Scottish notables were encouraged to sign their names in the Visitors' Book with outlandish hereditary titles revived for them from out of the shadows of the distant past: the Wolf of Badenoch, the Black Cock of the West and the Chief of the Children of the Mist, all made their way, sometimes to their surprise, to Easter Moncreiffe.

The crest of the Hays was a falcon, and before long Iain and Diana, now known familiarly as Puffin, had produced two sons, appropriately named Merlin and Peregrine. (As Iain put it in a letter, 'We are breeding falcons fast'.) They were followed by a clever, beautiful daughter, Alexandra.

Iain's whole attitude to nobility, and above all to genealogy, can be summed up in his dictum: 'We are not there to show off, but to add to the fun.' By this he meant that just as a piece of furniture or a picture takes on much more interest if you know its provenance, 'so does an individual the more the diverse ancestral elements that went to form him or her are known'. And without the existence of every single one of your antecedents, you would not have been *you*; you would have been somebody different. It is, to say the least, a perfectly logical and understandable point of view, even if it led Iain to somewhat outlandish extremes.

After studying law in Edinburgh, Iain was admitted to the Faculty of Advocates in 1950, and if his natural interests had lain in that direction would undoubtedly have prospered there, thanks to the clarity of his thought, his extraordinary memory and his capacity for intense and dogged study of anything that he considered important – for example his delighted discovery that Prince Charles is descended from Mary Queen of Scots not just seventeen times over, as Iain had previously estimated, but by no less than *twenty-two* lines of descent. However, what he considered important was very far removed from the day-to-day subjects on which people go to law and require advocates. Consequently, it comes as no surprise to learn that (in the words of a later senior law officer) 'he did not emerge as the sort of counsel that hard-headed Edinburgh practitioners are wont to instruct'. Much later, he also earned a DPhil at Edinburgh, and when he succeeded his cousin Sir David Moncreiffe of that Ilk as a baronet, and was asked by a Danish journalist why he preferred to be called Sir rather than Doctor, his perfectly reasonable answer was that 'that would be boasting, since I earned the doctorate myself, but as a baronet I am only a living memorial to a greater man'. 'Ilk', incidentally, means 'the same', signifying here that the family took its name from the place where it had lived since the beginning of recorded time, and probably, so Iain maintained, for a long time before. At one point a surprisingly well-informed member of the staff at Geneva Airport was heard to announce over the air that they were looking for Sir Iain Moncreiffe *'de la même chose'*, who had somehow got lost.

So his appearances in court were few, but his professional career as a Herald in the Court of Lord Lyon King of Arms made headway when he was appointed Falkland Pursuivant, and later promoted to the higher rank of Kintyre Pursuivant. For a time, too, he was Unicorn Pursuivant, and the Lord Lyon of the day took great pleasure in ringing him up at Easter Moncreiffe with the greeting 'Lyon here; is that you, Unicorn?' Iain was then promoted to Albany Herald in 1961, and for the next thirty years helped to arrange the State Ceremonies of Scotland, as well as having earlier attended the Coronation in Westminster Abbey, and the later royal visits to Edinburgh of the Kings of both Norway and Sweden. Throughout the 1970s he contributed reviews to a now extinct magazine called *Books and Bookmen*, which being consistently short of funds was always on the lookout for experts who would review books because they had something to say rather than to earn worthwhile fees. Iain had much to say: on one occasion his review of a life of Mary Queen of Scots ran to no less than 20,000 words, and was split up between three of the monthly issues. Iain had his extended fun and the magazine filled its pages; the attention of some readers may have flagged, but on the whole everyone was happy, which was so often Iain's chief object.

His historical obsessions, together with an unshakeable habit of burning the midnight oil, took their toll, and to his great sorrow his wife left him in 1964, and remarried. But by a phenomenal stroke of fortune he, too, remarried, two years later, a woman whose patience and calm were almost superhuman, and certainly had extraordinary demands made on them. Hermione Faulkner was eighteen years younger than Iain, and never, even under grave provocation, did she show signs of being ruffled by what to others might have seemed intolerable behaviour. In fact, the term 'unflappable' might have been coined to describe her, even after she suffered from a severe tumour and lost the sight of one eye. Nothing ever disturbed her unusual blend of natural dignity and modesty. Iain, too, in spite of occasional lapses, had strong feelings about the right way to behave. He was certainly never guilty of showing off: he never said anything for effect, but only because he had something to say which he considered worth saying. Even more remarkably, he never seemed to have an unkind word for anyone, even those who hacked away at everything he held sacred. Nor did he ever raise his voice or laugh loudly: a charming smile or a quiet chuckle was enough. And when thanked for his unflagging hospitality, instead of giving the impression that the thanks were earned, his modest acknowledgement took the form of the curious formula 'Woof, woof,' as of some gratified heraldic hound after a pat on the back. Indeed, after a visit to Chile, he took under his wing a retired Irish Guards mascot in the form of a very large wolfhound called O'Higgins, after the National Liberator and subsequent tyrant of that country.

In short, Iain had decided to live his life as a kind of self-appointed outpost of self-selected historical research, but with no university or foundation to support it. Frugal in everything except alcohol, hospitality and occasional travel, he earned almost nothing, but luckily lived through a period of prosperity for the members of Lloyd's, of which he was one. By the time that bubble burst, destroying many of those who depended on it, Iain was mercifully dead.

Natural History was of no special interest to him, though on one occasion he was able to cheer up a dinner neighbour (the daughter of one of his oldest friends) who was feeling down in the dumps before a Perth Ball, by whispering whimsically in her ear, 'Your trouble is you're descended from a baboon.' Her mood immediately lifted. And although not an ardent shooting man, he took sport in his stride when it came his way. On a visit to North Borneo in 1972, he went with his companions to see orang-utans being 'rehabilitated' in nests about sixty feet up in some gigantic trees. Ever on the lookout for a family resemblance, he recorded in his game book that 'they look just like Douglas-Homes.' On that occasion the bag consisted of about thirty leeches, none of which, however, attacked him successfully, though he recorded that 'the Colquhouns of Luss were covered in blood'. To quote once more from this esoteric volume, Iain attended at the age of eighteen a tiger shoot in Udaipur. He described the highlight of the day as follows: 'The Maharaja said, excitedly, "Shoot! Shoot! And I missed, missed." The beaters were two thousand spearmen and eighteen elephants, and the bag a single tiger. Next day, however, on an expedition after panther, an official with the title of Inspector of Dancing Girls shot a sow by mistake, and was deprived of his rifle for the rest of the day.

Enough has been said to show that Iain Moncreiffe fully deserved to be called eccentric. But the testimonials after his death in 1984, one of which described him as 'the last specimen of a long endangered species', underlined the qualities which, in spite of various disabilities and weaknesses, he was determined to live up to as far as he could. He never expected anything in return for his innumerable kindnesses, and the range and steadiness of his affection was astonishing. There were many whose imagination was stirred and stimulated by his generosity, and while there were a handful who took offence, he undoubtedly added to the interest as well as the pleasure and amusement of hundreds, perhaps thousands, of lives. Many have done worse.

*

Iain Moncreiffe was a researcher, obsessed with heredity but also full of good will towards men (and women). Another baronet, Sir Humphry Wakefield, is by contrast above all a man of action and of practical achievement. He deserves a high place among today's few eccentrics, for having fearlessly confronted a world in which the authorities concentrate so much of their time and misdirected energy on the dreary practice of dumbing down rather than lifting up. As Hugh Montgomery-Massingberd wrote in the *Daily Telegraph*, contrasting Humphry's restoration achievements with those of the anti-hero of *Yes Minister*: 'What the world badly needs is more Sir Humphrys and fewer Sir Humphreys.'

Humphry's earliest years were spent in the British Raj in India. His father Sir Edward was a brilliant classical scholar, a leader among the last generation to serve with real authority and inspiration in the Indian Civil Service, as Chief Minister in a series of Princely States before going to advise his cousin Field Marshal Wavell and then Lord Mountbatten on the political aspects of the dissolution. He and his wife were in Quetta at the time of the catastrophic earthquake in 1935. They survived by a miracle, but their six-year-old daughter and eighteen out of twenty of his official staff were killed.

Humphry was born just over a year later, and one can only guess at what effect these shattering circumstances had on his personality. Whatever it was, he grew up with a fierce determination to live up to the remarkable achievements, academic, athletic and political, of his immediate family and, especially, of his nineteenth-century forerunners. Perhaps the most surprising of them all was Edward Gibbon Wakefield (1796-1822): a wild prankster in his youth, he first eloped with a ward of court, who he adored but who died young. In a crazy attempt to replace her, he abducted an heiress and was consequently sent to prison in 1826 for three years. What he saw there changed him completely: starving young men hanged for stealing food; violent criminals deported, along with the weak, unlucky or useless, to penal colonies in Australia. In prison he wrote his chilling *Punishment by Death in the Metropolis*, which played a crucial part in the repeal of the Hanging Bill.

He next set himself the gigantic task of creating colonial settlements, at first in Australia, based on the basis of what was the very best in British civilisation. After founding Adelaide, which set the pattern for future Australian cities, he went to Canada where he inspired what later became the Durham Report, which reshaped British colonial policy. In 1839, he turned his attention to New Zealand, at a time when the French craved it as a penal colony; had it been established, it would, no doubt, have turned out even more savage than the English variety. Wellington was duly founded and administered by Edward's brother, Colonel William Wakefield, who had also gone to prison for abetting his brother's abduction; Nelson was discovered and later run by another brother, Captain Arthur Wakefield, famously killed in the Wairau Massacre. New Plymouth and Otago followed and, finally, Edward's dream of a Church of England settlement was achieved at Canterbury in 1848. A hundred and fifty years later, Humphry was to visit all these foundations for their anniversary celebrations.

Moving on to the twentieth century, Humphry's great-aunt Daisy Wakefield combined two triumphant careers, first as British High Diving Champion, and later as a colourful missionary in the Sahara, where she formulated a written version of the Touareg language, and translated the Bible into it. Her brother Arthur, a boxing champion, was also, a missionary, but in Newfoundland. He also joined the first ever attempt on Everest in 1922, which set out with the most rudimentary equipment, reached a spot within half a mile of the summit, but was driven back by avalanches which swept seven of its members to their deaths. Later in the 1920s, Humphry's Uncle Wavell, later Lord Wakefield, was perhaps the most distinguished all-round athlete of his day: a champion sprinter, he also captained England at Rugby, and appropriately inflicted the first defeat of the all-powerful New Zealand side on their home ground. Wavell saw action as a pilot in both world wars, having got off to a good start at the age of seventeen by being the first to land an aeroplane on the deck of a battleship; a feat for which he was much applauded, but also court-martialled.

One way and another, there was much for Humphry to live up to. Sent back from India at the age of eight, he went through the gruelling system at Gordonstoun with credit. Joint Guardian (captain) of the school and captain of rugby for two seasons, he was also captain of hockey and squash as well as president of debating, art and (hardly surprisingly) dramatics. As senior cadet in the Air Corps he was instrumental in linking it with the Air Force Mountain Rescue Service. This eventually led to his becoming President of the Northumbrian Fell and Mountain Rescue Service, and Patron of the International Search Research Centre for behavioural patterns in lost people. But he also found time for music and riding. He is now a Director of the Spoleto Music Festival, but also won many equestrian events at an early age, and later won a famous seven-mile horse race outside Madrid in record time. This he achieved by the simple method of swimming a river on his obliging horse, and cutting two miles off the distance to be covered. (There was nothing in the rules against it.) But what gave him even greater satisfaction was to catch a runaway horse, with a tinker's cart behind it, galloping down the Cromwell Road in London. He pursued it, over some discouraging traffic lights, on his motor-cycle, and somehow managed to lean over and catch its reins before gently bringing it to a halt. Later, his rescue of another escaped horse and carriage in Chicago brought him handsome headlines.

Academic distinction at Gordonstoun was rare, to say the least, and when Humphry won a county scholarship to Cambridge the school was given a half-holiday. Before going up, he was given a national service commission in the Tenth Hussars, and saw action in the Middle East in the tense days of the Suez Crisis in 1956, mounting an unorthodox rescue of a group of officers who had been kidnapped and incarcerated in a mud fort in the desert. At Cambridge, he was determined to avoid the classics, in which his family had achieved successes that could hardly have been equalled. Instead, he was able to read an unusual mixture of biology and anthropology, archaeology and English Literature. He also played rugby for the university, but without gaining a blue.

Joining the furniture department at Christies in London, he devised their first sales of musical instruments, as well as their first ethnographic sale, which dispersed the collection of Jacob Epstein. After two years at Christies he left for Malletts, where among other things he was put in charge of the craftsmen and their workshops. He developed an acute fascination for their work, which was to have important consequences. Through the family of his wife, a daughter of Viscount De L'Isle, VC, KG, he paid several visits to a romantic, ruined castle called Lough Cutra, in Galway, formerly the home of the Gort family. It had been designed by Nash, but had been abandoned by the family and the Irish Government as being too far gone, and too expensive to repair. Humphry thought otherwise, and within two years the work of rebuilding was accomplished, entirely thanks, as he has recorded, to a team of four outstanding craftsmen, all called Michael, who could (and did with great enthusiasm) turn their hands to anything from recreating decorative plasterwork to replacing collapsed staircases and installing central heating. Angry planning officials threatened lawsuits, but when the smoke cleared away

Humphry emerged as an adviser to the local government on tourist development, and was even awarded the first ever public money to be provided in support of a private venture.

At this stage, Humphry's marriage came to an end, and he was invited by Malletts to open a shop for them in New York. The Michaels, as they were known, had bravely followed him there and were responsible for restoring magnificent pieces of furniture, which was sold to major collectors in New York, and to museums all over the United States. But they also found time for building work. Humphry designed, and the Michaels created, what were later described as large-scale 'architectless, planningless, permissionless houses', including a barn-style complex of houses in Maine for the then US Ambassador to Moscow, Thomas J. Watson Jr. The ancient timbers of the central barn were moved bodily from Connecticut across 'bridges which were too frail, and ferries that were too small'. But they reached their destination.

Humphry decided that this sort of thing was more fun than being a shopkeeper. He designed a house in Dublin for the dress designer Sybil Connolly; then back he came to London, to design a brand-new house in Kensington to contain the offices of the Portsmouth & Sunderland group of newspapers. He was highly diverted when the building won two 'restoration' awards, in spite of being built from scratch. They did indeed use old gates, columns, cobbles and metal-work, but they certainly followed no previous design. He then launched the team on the business of copying important historic pieces of furniture, including items from Blenheim, Wilton, Chatsworth, and Penshurst, and later from the Hermitage and other imperial palaces in Russia. The next advance was into the field of porcelain, in which one original piece was sold to the Metropolitan Museum for one million dollars. The development of these plans, and others involving textiles, and gold and silver objects, was made possible when the business became the property of a major American manufacturer: the combined annual retail turnover has since risen to $50m.

All through these years Humphry was indulging in a truly eccentric, but in due course immensely rewarding and successful enterprise. The forebears of his third wife, the Grey family, had formerly owned, for several centuries, Chillingham Castle in Northumberland, a huge medieval fortress, described by Sir Walter Scott as bearing 'the true rust of the Barons' wars', but by then in the last stages of decay. Undaunted by what appeared to others, including his in-laws, to be a crazy and moreover impossible task, he applied his formidable energy and powers of persuasion to carrying out something at the prospect of which both the National Trust and English Heritage had thrown up their hands in horror. Wisely, he kept his plans to himself, and the respective families only learnt that he had acquired Chillingham when they read it in the newspapers. He immediately invited the public to share his fascination with 'rot and repair', and 25,000 visitors paid their entrance money in the first year. The work still goes on, and the number of visitors has been maintained, thanks not only to the remarkable restoration that has taken place, but also to a wide collection of Wakefield memorabilia connected with the family's various achievements, which has been assembled there. The garden, too, has been restored, to reveal its Wyattville design, and the castle plays host to various regional charitable events of which Humphry is either patron or president, not the least of which is the Avison Ensemble, a group of classical musicians who use instruments made in their original styles, and reach audiences that would never otherwise hear them. There is something Leonardoesque about the mixture which Humphry distilled between design, mechanical development and artistic inspiration, and Chillingham bears witness to all three.

But before time's winged chariot should catch up with him, Humphry decided that there were still some physical exploits to be

181

fitted in. One chance came when he was in New Zealand for the hundred and fiftieth anniversary of the tall ships arriving at Nelson. The 1992 New Zealand National Mount Everest expedition team was training by making their first ascent of Mount Wakefield (named, needless to say, after yet another member of the family). He naturally decided to join them, and an invitation followed to accompany them to the Himalayas, under the heroic and tragic Everest hand Rob Hall. Their adventures were hair-raising, but disaster was fortunately averted.

One final expedition was to accompany the great American hero Colonel Norman Vaughan to the Antarctic, the last on which husky dogs were to be used. The object was to make the first ever ascent of Mount Vaughan, which had been named after the Colonel when he had acted as dog driver to Admiral Byrd, the great pioneering antarctic explorer, in 1928. What was astonishing about this project, even by Wakefield standards, was that the Colonel was now in his ninetieth year, and was being sponsored to climb his mountain by the National Geographic Magazine. Total disaster was only narrowly avoided. An aeroplane loaded with members of the expedition, with their dogs and supplies, crashed in the ice, but the team was mercifully rescued. The following year, the Colonel returned, though without Humphry, and triumphantly climbed his mountain. A few years later in 2000, Humphry enrolled on an expedition to the North Pole, but a heart bypass operation tiresomely intervened. However, he still gets vicarious excitement from the exploits of his eldest son as a formula racing driver, while his second son flourishes in the tangled thickets of the New York art world, and his daughter acts as assistant editor of *The Spectator*. He has recently stolen back, with great ingenuity, his white Mercedes from the thieves who stole it from him in London. One has the feeling that there is more to come.

Notes for further reading

Besides books referred to in the text, the following provide
further information

Col. Sibthorpe is well described in John Michell's *Eccentric Lives and Peculiar Notions* (Thames and Hudson 1984), as is his brother Richard Sibthorpe in *Two Studies in Virtue* by Christopher Sykes (Collins, 1953). There is an excellent biography of Aubrey Herbert, *The Man Who Was Greenmantle*, by his granddaughter Margaret FitzHerbert (OUP, 1985). Wilfrid Blunt's biography, *John Christie of Glyndebourne*, (Bles 1968) is a competent and lively study. The best book on Beckford is by James Lees-Milne, *William Beckford*, (Century 1990) sadly out of print except in a paperback edition with a defective index. There are many lives and critical studies of Blake, easily traced. Sir George Sitwell wrote a number of recondite booklets himself: *On the Making of Gardens* was reprinted along with other material in *Hortus Sitwellianus*, edited by his grandson, Sir George Sitwell (Michael Russell 1984), but now out of print. His daughter Edith wrote a book called *The English Eccentrics* (Penguin 1971). The style is fanciful and dated, but some notable characters are described.

Besides the lives of Lady Hester Stanhope quoted, her niece the Duchess of Cleveland wrote *The Life and Letters of Lady Hester Stanhope* for private circulation in 1903. Many of Sir Iain Moncreiffe's long book reviews are collected in *A Moncreiffe Miscellany*, edited by Hugh Montgomery Massingberd, and his masterly book *The Highland Clans* (Barrie & Jenkins 1982) is to be reissued shortly. Victoria Woodhull is described, rather solemnly, in *The Woman Who Ran for President*, by Lois Beechey Underhill, published in America by Bridge Works Publishing Co., Bridghampton, New York.